JOY NWOSU LO-BAMIJOKO

The Saga of a Nigerian Female Ethnomusicologist

GODWIN SADOH

BESTSELLING AUTHOR ON AMAZON

iUniverse LLC
Bloomington

Joy Nwosu Lo-Bamijoko
The Saga of a Nigerian Female Ethnomusicologist

iUniverse books may be ordered through booksellers or by contacting:

iUniverse
1663 Liberty Drive
Bloomington, IN 47403
www.iuniverse.com
1-800-Authors (1-800-288-4677)

ISBN: 978-1-4697-8586-8 (sc)
ISBN: 978-1-4697-8587-5 (e)

Printed in the United States of America

iUniverse rev. date: 03/12/2014

Contents

Prologue

My first encounter with Joy Nwosu Lo-Bamijoko goes far back to 1977. It was the year of the World Black Festival of Arts and Culture—FESTAC, that took place in Lagos. I vividly remember watching Joy on TV perform at the National Theater and the National Stadium; both nestled in Lagos, the former federal capital of Nigeria. With eyes glued to the TV screen for several days, I and my sisters were mesmerized by her stunning and flamboyant performances. This was our first time of seeing Joy and hearing her beautiful voice. We have never heard a woman's voice sounded so refined and pure. I can still recollect my sisters spoofing her flawless high tessitura that she climaxed effortlessly several times. Although, we did not know her until then, but our late mother already knew Joy from her radio shows and recorded LP songs. When Joy appeared on TV, our mother was the one who gave us a lot of background information about Joy and she even sang some of her favorite songs from the LP records. She had so many wonderful things to say about Joy. From that day, I have been following the career of Joy on several plains—TV and radio shows, concerts, and even bumped into her at some of the Nigerian Musicological Society conferences that took place at various universities.

I have had deep admiration and respect for Joy's career as a teacher, performer, and scholar. Even though I was oblivious of the plan to write a book on her life in the future, I began collecting documents on Joy's work way back in Nigeria out of keen interest. It was in fall 2010 that I came to realize that I had collected enough materials on Joy's work and would like to develop them into a book. When I contacted her and shared my thoughts with her, Joy gladly accepted, and even sent me more documents and photos dating back to her early musical activities at Enugu in the 1960s.

Apart from knowing Joy very well from my teens, there are other factors that motivated me to write a book on her. First, Joy was the first professionally trained female musician in Nigeria to cross-over from Western classical style to indigenous pop music, and successfully combine the two musical genres; second, Joy was the first female trained musician to set up a dance band in Nigeria; third, Joy was the first trained female musician to release a Long Playing record in Nigeria; fourth, she deserves recognition for her trailblazing efforts to liberate Nigerian women from subjugation by their men counterparts; fifth, Joy was the most hardworking and most productive among her female contemporaries; finally, I am intrigued by Joy's resilience and determination to flourish in the very purviews that were exclusively dominated by men, and her impressive triumphs over most of the obstacles thrown at her to truncate her ambitions. For all these extraordinary virtues, I concluded that a treatise must be written on this infrangibly, indefatigable, and feisty woman, to promote her accomplishments around the globe and preserve her legacy for future generations to study and emulate.

Chapter 1

The Biography of Joy Nwosu Lo-Bamijoko

Joy Ifeoma Nroli Nwosu Lo-Bamijoko is a highly educated, articulate, savvy, and versatile musician with interests covering every area of musical specializations, including operatic singing, popular music, piano and traditional musical instruments, music education, music criticism, teaching, African ethnomusicology, dancing, broadcasting, skits writing and acting, choral conducting, and song writing. She was the most gifted professionally trained Nigerian female musician; and apparently, the most productive female scholar, who had distinguished herself in her native country and internationally as an authority on Nigerian music. Earning her Ph.D. in Music Education with emphasis on African ethnomusicology in 1981 from the University of Michigan, Ann Arbor, made her the second Nigerian woman to receive a doctorate in music.

Formative Years at Enugu

Joy was born on 27 August, 1940, in Enugu, Anambra State of southeast Nigeria. Her parents were Charles Belonwu and Deborah Nwosu. Joy is the fifth in rank of the seven children of her parents. Joy was born into a musical family. Her father was a Faith Tabernacle Church pastor, organist, and baritone singer; while her mother sang alto in the same church choir—she's got the pedigree. Indeed, Joy was surrounded by various musical activities and was introduced to music at a very tender age by singing with her parents at the Faith Tabernacle Church Choir. As a child, her father took her everywhere he went. Out of all his seven children, he named her Nroli—the chosen one. He would perch her at the organ bench close to him, while he played, and she would swung her legs, and sung in high pitched voice with the choir. All these experiences served as her early contacts with European music thereby developing her interest and taste for European classical music. The more exposure Joy received, the more her ears grew accustomed to music pitches, scales, intonations, timbres, choral and organ repertoires.

In her early teens, Joy joined the Saint Bartholomew's Church Choir, Enugu, where she sang, participated and won several choir competitions. It was at this church that she received her first lessons in music. While in the choir, she learned to sing in tonic sol-fa, and to transcribe songs orally to tonic sol-fa. Joy was tutored by both the senior choir members and section leaders who were advanced in reading music and who were at the same time saddled with the responsibility of teaching the rudiments of music to new choristers.

Between 1958 and 1961, Joy attended the Holy Rosary College, Enugu, where she obtained the Grade II Teacher's Certificate upon graduation. Outside of the choir, there was no formal music curriculum at the institution. While in the college choir, Joy taught her co-members the tonic sol-fa skills she had acquired from Saint Bartholomew's Church. The Sisters gave Joy free access to the piano, but there was no instructor to teach her to play the instrument. Joy would later receive formal piano lessons in Rome. During her student days at Holy Rosary College, Joy represented her school in the then Eastern Nigerian Festival of the Arts and won first place prizes in the soprano competitions consecutively for seven years. Whenever Joy mounts the stage, the other contestants did not have a chance of winning. Paradoxically, she did not know at the time that she was going to become a professional singer. To her, singing was just something she enjoyed doing and gave her intense pleasure.

Joy Nwosu Receives a Farewell Book Gift from the Enugu Choral Society, 1960.

Joy Nwosu Sings at the Festival Gala Night, 1960.

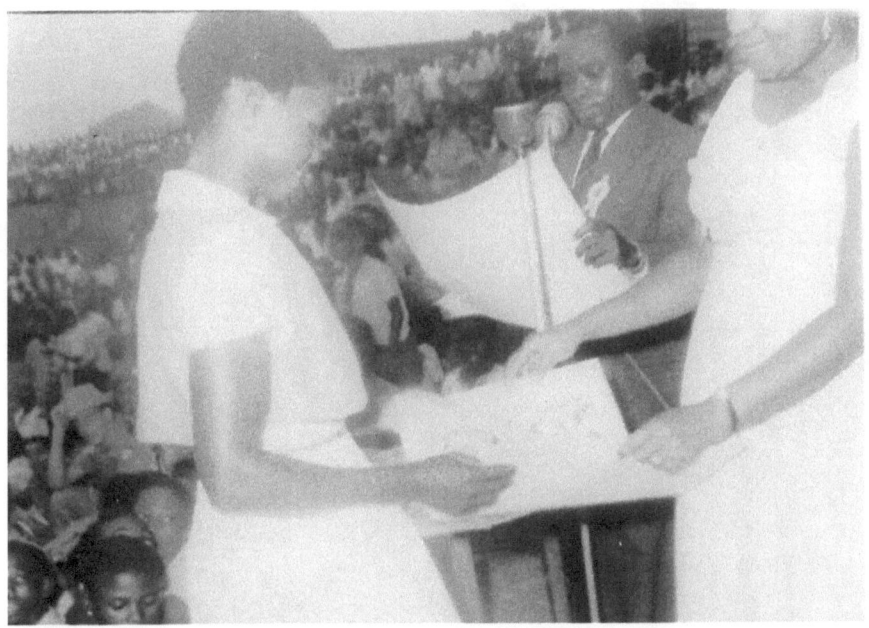

Joy Nwosu Receives a Certificate of Merit from Mrs. Flora Azikiwe,[1] for First Place in Soprano, Festival of the Arts, Enugu, 1960.

1   Flora Azikiwe was the very First Lady of Nigeria in the 1960s, during her husband's term as the first civilian President of the Federal Republic of Nigeria, from 1960 to 1966.

Joy Nwosu with College Best Friend, Caroline, 1960.

Joy Nwosu with College Best Friend and a Cousin, 1961.

At this tender age, Joy had already started assuming prominent roles in operatic productions. For instance, she was Nanki Poo in the *Mikado* by W. S. Gilbert and Sir Arthur Sullivan, performed at the Holy Rosary College to celebrate Nigeria's independence in 1960. Her brilliant performance motivated the Holy Rosary Sisters to offer her scholarship to study music at the Royal College of Music, Dublin, Ireland. Joy recounts some of the pleasant memories at the college and commended her teachers who encouraged her to develop her musical aptitudes:

> I attended a Convent School. While in that school, we had a Sister, Mary Aina, I am not sure that is the correct spelling of her name, but we pronounced that name as "Onyia." She was the musical one. Sister Aina was very strict and wanted everyone to be as good as she was. I did not like her much, because she drove us like slaves. I sang and tried to excel in singing only to get her off my back. The Principal, Sister Mary Edwards, on the other hand, was a darling spirit. She too was strict, but caring. She did not sing, however, she encouraged those of us who sang. She was proud of my accomplishments. After graduation, she retained me to teach music and arithmetic in the school. I am sure she was behind the scholarship I was granted by their Order.

Joy Nwosu in the Wedding Scene in the *Mikado*, at Holy Rosary College, Enugu, 1960.

Nanki Poo—Joy, kisses Yum Yum in the *Mikado*, at Holy Rosary College, Enugu, 1960.

The Engagement Scene in the *Mikado*, at Holy Rosary College, Enugu, 1960.

Joy Nwosu's Graduation Photo with St. Theresa House Girls at Holy Rosary College, Enugu, 1961.

St. Theresa House Wins the Silver Cup at Holy Rosary College, Enugu, 1961.

**Joy Nwosu and Graduating Class in Traditional Attire at Holy
Rosary College, Enugu, 1961.**

Graduating Class with Sister Mary Edward, the Principal at Holy Rosary College, Enugu, 1961.

Joy Nwosu as a Teacher at Holy Rosary College, Enugu, 1962.

Joy Nwosu and Members of the Enugu Choral Society, Farewell Photo, 1962.

Joy Nwosu on Her Way to Rome, 1962.

Professional Training in Italy

The then Eastern Nigerian Government annulled the scholarship offer from the Holy Rosary College and awarded its own scholarship to send Joy to study in Rome. The government had a vague premonition that the Holy Sisters wanted to use their scholarship to lure Joy into the Sisterhood. Joy, on the other hand, perceived the scholarship awards differently. Joy thought they gave her the awards to get her out of the singing competitions. With her presence at the competitions, nobody else had the chance to shine or even win. Joy also thought that they wanted new talents to spring up, without her adumbrating them all the time.

In the light of this personal deducing, Joy proceeded in 1962 to study music at various conservatories of music in Italy with the scholarship award from the Eastern Nigerian Government, given to her in recognition of her outstanding performances at the Eastern Nigerian Festival of Arts. Any family would be enraptured at such good news and Joy's family was no exception. They had only one reservation; they were not impressed with Joy's choice of a career in music. In those days, music was perceived as suitable for drop-outs, lazy people, paupers, and was looked upon as a profession for the recalcitrant. Her family tried to dissuade Joy from pursuing music, but the scholarship board did not condescend to their pressure. Ironically, prior to the award, Joy had no idea of the career she wanted to pursue; hence, the offer turns out to be an epiphany that clarified her thoughts. Joy later discovered that she loved the idea of studying music.

Joy Nwosu at Perugia School of Italian Language in Italy, 1962.

Joy Nwosu at a Flea Market in Rome, 1963.

Joy Nwosu on a Field Trip with Her Hostel Sisters in Rome, 1963.

Joy went to Rome in 1962 with one big ambition, to study and become an operatic singer. She was fortunate to be admitted into one of the world's best schools in vocal performance. However, the admission was temporarily logjam, because she had to first enroll for three months at the Perugia School of Italian Language in Italy. The language school prepared her for taking classes in the conservatory since classes were taught exclusively in the Italian language. Having conquered the language barrier, Joy went on to audition for admission to the Conservatorio Di Musica, Santa Cecilia in Rome, and she was accepted to study voice. In that school, Joy developed the discipline and daily routine to practice, that is, one hour for voice and four hours devoted to piano. This left her with very little time for socializing, but Joy found time to attend concerts and watch operatic productions.

Attending opera shows was part of the requirement for vocal studies at the conservatory. Her voice professor was so impressed with Joy that she gave Joy title roles in two major operas, in a land that created this style of music. In 1966, Joy sang Turandot in Puccini's opera of that name in the Garden Theater of Castel Gondolfo, and in 1972, she sang excerpts from Verdi's great opera, *Aida*, at the Barberini Theater in Rome. This was a great accomplishment and honor bestowed upon a black woman from the continent of Africa. Joy also performed widely all over Europe, including Rome, Florence, Milan, Dublin, and London.

Joy Nwosu in Concert with Her Voice Teacher in Rome, 1966.

While in Italy, Joy studied for five years at the Conservatori Di Musica, Santa Cecilia in Rome; Luigi Perugini in Florence; and Giacchino Perugini in Pesaro, all nestled in Italy. Not relenting on her efforts, Joy felt it would be an asset to have knowledge of communication studies, since at that time Nigeria was yet to boast of a proper theatre. Joy therefore took a course in mass communication and specialized in cinematography, for another two years at the International University for Social Studies in Rome. Joy spent a total of ten years away from Nigeria (1962-1972), out of which eight years was invested in her education in Italy at several conservatories of music. The last two years of Joy's sojourn, 1970 to 1972, was spent as a refugee of the Biafra Civil War[2] beginning in Ivory Coast, West Africa. In 1970, Caritas Internazionale sent Joy to Abidjan in Ivory Coast to organize a sort of school for the Biafra kids who were evacuated there from Nigeria. The mission was short-lived because Joy, an Igbo woman from the southeast of Nigeria, was a proponent of the Igbo secession against the Federal Republic of Nigeria. Joy often made incendiary statements about the war. Unknown to her, these rants put her life in extreme danger. News about Joy's stance on the war quickly got to some Biafra Army chiefs taking refuge in Ivory Coast at the time. Based on the sensitivity of the scoop, the chiefs had a premonition of a looming danger on Joy's life; hence, they moved swiftly to get Joy out of the refugee camp for fear that she could be hurt. The army chiefs whisked Joy away at night from the camp to London, England. Back in London, Joy spent some months doing odd jobs to survive. She lived with her uncle, his wife, and children. Eventually, Joy returned to Rome later in 1970, resolved to make significant progress in her career. While in Rome, she started writing and got her first two books published, and she also established a small batik business. Things were beginning to look good for Joy when suddenly she received

---

2   The Biafra civil war took place in Nigeria from 1967 to 1970. The Igbo of the southeast region engaged in secession against the Federal Republic of Nigeria, in particular, the northern oligarchy. This eerie period witnessed a myriad of lackadaisical cadavers mostly in the northern and eastern regions of Nigeria.

a message from Nigeria that her mother was dying at home. Joy left everything behind in Rome and boarded the next flight to Nigeria in mid 1972. At the end of her studies in Italy, Joy had earned several diplomas in music:

1. Voice Diploma: Conservatorio Di Musica, Santa Cecilia, Rome, Italy (1962-1965).
2. Diploma, Summa Cum Lode, in Mass Communication, Specialization in Cinematography: Universita Internazionale Per I Studi Sociali, Pro-Deo, Rome, Italy (1966-1968).
3. Licentiate in Music Theory: Conservatorio Di Musica, Luigi Peruggini, Florence, Italy (1967).
4. Voice Diploma: Conservatorio Di Musica, Gioacchino Perugini, Pesaro, Italy (1970).

Joy considers the years spent abroad studying, a worthwhile experience: "At the time I went abroad, there was nowhere to study music in Nigeria. All of us first generation music educated Nigerians had to study abroad. It was a gratifying experience. It fine-tuned my musical preferences so much that when I started writing my own original folk songs, they stylistically differ from the traditional folk songs. I had to classify them as contemporary folk songs, to be sung with 'cultured voice'." Joy was one of the first Nigerians and perhaps, one of the first Africans to study music in Italy.

Professional Career in Nigeria—Phase One

Joy returned to Nigeria from Italy at the age of thirty-one. From the 1960s to 1970s, most Nigerian musicians trained abroad often commence their professional career at the Nigerian Broadcasting Corporation—NBC, because there were not too many jobs for professional musicians in those days. Therefore, it was not surprising upon her return to Nigeria in 1972, that Joy was appointed to the position of Producer of Music Programs at the Nigerian Broadcasting Corporation in Lagos. She recounts some of her memorable programs and experiences at the Nigerian Broadcasting Corporation and the Nigerian Television Authority—NTA:

My years at NBC Lagos started in mid-1972 and ended in 1975. I was a music producer. I was told to invent myself with the program. The only format to the program was that you had to choose a theme that will enable you to talk to your listeners, and intermittently play a piece of music to break the monotony of your voice. I decided to focus my theme on the elderly, those too old to be out and about, who rely on the radio to see the outside world. I would talk to them as if I were in their home visiting them. When I started to get lots of feed-backs from the elderly, I knew I was on the right path. While broadcasting, I was also running my band. I did my first recording with Decca in my first year at NBC, and when that song, "UWAM," exploded on the airwaves that morning, my life changed, and my name became a house-hold name in Nigeria. People who knew me then still remember that moment. It was a magical moment that was best described as 'out of this world.' To hear my own voice on the air for the first time, I could not relate to that person. In fact, that has been my attitude toward my several performances since then. Indeed, the radio publicity established my reputation nationally in Nigeria. When I went to work every day, I was easily recognized by my fans, and I will simply shrug, and keep going. I did not like the limelight at all. Too bad my job put me right there on the spot. Because of the close relationship between NBC and NTA, I also performed regularly on television. My first television program was produced by Art Alade, while my piano accompanist for the show was the late Ayo Bankole. I got to the television station on time for the program, but as usual, Ayo was not there. He was never good at keeping time, but he will be there. Art started fretting, because it was supposed to be a live program. Art wanted to peruse the songs to see whether he could accompany me; that put me into frenzy. How could Art accompany me when he did not practice with me? Rather than let him mess me up, I decided to mess myself up. As soon as it was time for me to go on air, I told Art not to bother, and simply asked him to point the camera on me; he did, and I did what I do best. I sang and accompanied myself on the piano on live television show, and I even surprised myself. Art could not believe his eyes and ears; he was gobsmacked. At the end of the program, Ayo quietly walked in and learned that the program was over. The next day, that program was the talk of the town. I ran over to the television station to request a copy of my show, but alas! They had recorded another program over it. I did not believe them, of course, but that was the story I was told. After FESTAC[3] in 1977, choral music exploded in Nigeria. Many music graduates, especially from our universities, were either setting up their own choirs or singing with existing choirs. The Laz Ekwueme National Chorale was going strong. I was directing the Christ Our Light Catholic Choir on UNILAG campus. We had choir competitions in Lagos, and many choirmasters sought me for help with their choirs. In 1982, when I returned to Lagos after my doctoral studies in Michigan, I started working privately with some of the church choirmasters in Lagos. By 1983, the demand was so much that I decided to take my teaching to the television, so that I could reach a wider audience. It was a weekly program, I believe every Tuesday at 6:00 PM, when I was sure my students would have been back from work. My private students were my targeted audience. At this point, I stopped presenting my choir for competitions, and became a judge at the choral competitions. I taught basic music elements, rudiments, voice production, and conducting. I also took the opportunity of the competitions to give the competing choirs and their choirmasters, short lessons on singing and conducting. My show was the first show ever at the National Theater, a constant beehive of artistic productions. I performed with my band at the inauguration and commissioning of the National Theater. I performed in three different idioms: my folk songs, art songs, and a sketch—skit. Yes, I also did sketches. I used to write and perform short sketches between songs. The one I staged on that

---

3   FESTAC is the acronym for the World Festival of the Black Arts and Culture that took place in Lagos, Nigeria, in 1977.

day was titled, "Waiting for the Bus." My greatest regret today, is that I do not have recordings of my performances. There were so many that I would have loved to have.

Joy Nwosu at the Nigerian Television Authority—NTA, Lagos, 1973.

Joy occupied the position of Producer of Music Programs at the Nigerian Broadcasting Corporation in Lagos, until she was appointed Music Lecturer II on 15 April, 1975, at the Department of Music, University of Lagos. When she got hired as a lecturer by the University of Lagos, Joy applied to Radio Nigeria for a transfer to UNILAG, but her requisition was denied. Her then boss vowed that the only way she could leave was to resign. The bane of contention was that he was shocked that Joy could get such a prestigious position at the university with what he thought was inadequate credentials. The truth of the matter was a clear case of envy and rivalry common in Nigeria among professional musicians; because her boss, trained in Europe, also had music diplomas like Joy. He could not fathom how Joy was hired for a steep position that he desperately wanted to boost his ego and further his career in the academia. In addition, he returned to Nigeria from Europe over a decade before Joy arrived from Italy. Since academic appointment was often done by seniority, he thought he should have been given the job. Joy believed he was the mastermind behind the conspiracy to impede her chances of getting the lofty position at UNILAG.

Politicking and Rancor at the University of Lagos

On arrival at the University of Lagos campus, Joy's first two years at the institution were good. Her colleagues, Lazarus Ekwueme and late Ayo Bankole,[4] were happy to see her join them. Joy had already made a name for herself as Joy Nwosu—the canny voice on radio waves. Bankole and Joy collaborated in several concerts. Bankole was very close to Joy. He played a remarkable role in establishing Joy's operatic singing career as her proficient piano accompanist at several concerts. Bankole also helped Joy to keep her job at UNILAG while some of her colleagues connived to get her fired. Joy recounts Bankole's inexorable support for her with deep admiration and gratitude: "Ayo Bankole was a very lovable person, upright and just. He respected me as much as I respected him. He was my piano accompanist when he was alive. We

---

4   For further readings on Ayo Bankole, see Godwin Sadoh, *Intercultural Dimensions in Ayo Bankole's Music* (New York: iUniverse Publishing, 2007).

performed in concerts and on television together. When he wrote the *FESTAC Cantata,* he made me his lead soprano… Ayo was the only one among my contemporaries that understood and respected my Italian training. Others trivialized it and did everything within their power to sidetrack me…"[5]

---

5   Godwin Sadoh, *Intercultural Dimensions in Ayo Bankole's Music* (New York: iUniverse Publishing, 2007), 39.

Ayo Bankole at the Italian Embassy in Lagos, 1972.

Akin Euba later joined the music faculty at UNILAG. According to Joshua Uzoigwe, Euba left the University of Ife—now Obafemi Awolowo University, in 1977 as Acting Head of the Department of Music, and took up appointment as the Director of the Center for Cultural Studies at the University of Lagos, in the same year. Euba was appointed full Professor of Music at the Center for Cultural Studies in 1978.[6] Joy was tremendously enthusiastic when Euba joined the faculty, and was planning for the great things they could do together. Joy made frantic efforts to love all her colleagues because they were all great men in music. She felt honored to be among them.

Unfortunately, the pristine atmosphere quickly gave way to an ominous bank of dark clouds in the university. It all started in 1976 while Bankole was still alive, but intensified with the arrival of Euba. Rumors started filtering on campus that Joy was not qualified to be a lecturer at the institution. The top professors at the Faculty of Arts started putting pressure on Bankole and Euba to expose Joy. Ekwueme was left out of the loop because he was considered to be her mentor and the one instrumental in getting Joy hired at UNILAG. Consequently, Ekwueme kept Joy abreast of the fiasco.

At that time, they had a benign man as the Vice Chancellor of UNILAG, world renowned Professor of African History, Jacob Festus Ade Ajayi;[7] a true personification of a Good Samaritan and a beacon

---

6   Joshua Uzoigwe, *Akin Euba: An Introduction to the Life and Music of a Nigerian Composer* (Bayreuth: Eckhard Breitinger, 1992), 26-27.

7   Prof. Jacob Festus Ade Ajayi was the Vice Chancellor of the University of Lagos from 1972 to 1978, and Professor Emeritus of History at the University of Ibadan, where he also served as Acting Vice Chancellor. His awards include several honorary degrees from universities such as Leicester, 1975; Birmingham, 1984; and Ondo State University, 1992. He has also been appointed Honorary Fellow, School of Oriental and African Studies (SOAS), London, 1994; Foundation Fellow of the Historical Society of Nigeria, 1980; Corresponding Fellow of the Royal Historical Society of Britain, 1979; Nigerian National order of Merit, October, 1986; Ondo State Role of Honor, 1989. In 1987, Prof. Ajayi was presented with the 25th Anniversary Gold medal at the University of Lagos. He has also received the Distinguished Africanist Award, 1993; UNESCO

in a storm of hurt. Joy went to him to complain about the innuendo, and to inform him that she was ready to go to the United States to pursue a Ph.D. in order to halt the scoop. By this time, Ekwueme had also become a Professor of Music.[8] Prof. Ade Ajayi rather suggested to Joy that she should consider doing her Ph.D. at UNILAG, under the supervision of the two Professors of Music. Ekwueme was pessimistic of such a rambunctious enterprise that was already steeped in skepticism, but Euba was blunt and did not mince words with Joy. Simply put, Euba went cold turkey. He did not believe that Joy was qualified for admission to a Bachelor's program, how much more a Ph.D. in music.

Avicenna Silver Medal for outstanding contribution to the General History of Africa (1964-1999); Order of the Federal Republic of Nigeria (OFR), 2000; and most distinguished Alumnus Awards (MDA), University of Ibadan, 2001. His traditional titles are Babapitan of Ikole-Ekiti, January 1983, and Onikoyi of Ife, April 1983.

8   The first three Nigerians to be appointed professors of music were Fela Sowande, Akin Euba, and Lazarus Ekwueme respectively. Sowande was appointed professor at Howard University, Washington, DC, in 1968.

Professor Jacob Festus Ade Ajayi.

The Conspiracy

Euba surreptitiously followed up his appraisal of Joy's Italian credentials translated by himself at the Italian Embassy in Lagos. Euba sought the Italian Ambassador to ratify his assessment. Ironically, Euba did not speak Italian, nor did he understand the Italian system of rating their credentials. The clandestine ploy was foiled by the Italian Ambassador, who knew Joy quite well because she was a regular performer at the embassy in Lagos. Having determined to extricate Joy from those ravenous wolves, the Ambassador sent his own car to chauffeur her from UNILAG to the embassy.

On arrival at the embassy, the Ambassador informed Joy of Euba's conniving with another lady, and how they had attempted to convince him to validate Euba's translation and assessment of Joy's credentials. "Of course I refused to sign his papers." The Ambassador told Joy. "I told him that we have a department in Italy that deals with certificate assessments, and he should send the credentials there for proper evaluation if he really wanted to know the truth about your qualifications. Now, my advice to you is to leave that place if they do not believe in you." Joy left the embassy in shock and determined to follow the Ambassador's advice; but luck was on her side. It was 1977as FESTAC was just winding down, that the United States Embassy in Lagos offered a number of exchange visitor scholarships to some Nigerian artists; interestingly, Joy was fortunate to be one of the privileged recipients. Accordingly, in a bid to silence her critics and salvage her job, Joy resorted to visit the United States to apply and audition for graduate schools.

Joy Nwosu at FESTAC '77at the Main Bowl Auditorium of the National Theater, Lagos, 1977.

Months after Joy returned from the United States, she received a letter of admission to a doctoral program in music education from the University of Michigan, Ann Arbor. She was finally vindicated and ecstatic! Joy first ran to Ekwueme with her letter. After reading it, Ekwueme asked whether she had shown it to Euba; she said no, but that she was going to do so immediately. By this time, Euba treated Joy like a pest that had to be eradicated from the community. He refused to return her greetings whenever she greeted him. Joy was not perturbed and refused to be distracted by such frivolous antics. She went on to knock on Euba's door, opened it, and entered. Joy had a broad smile on her face, but he scowled at her. "I want you to see this." Joy told him, handing Euba her admission letter. While he read it, Joy watched his countenance for reactions. Euba placed the letter quietly on his desk, stood up, and offered Joy his hand and said, "Congratulations colleague."[9] Joy took the letter from his desk, folded it, and walked out of his office with her head held high.

Indeed, the recognition and acceptance of Joy's credentials as being sufficient enough for admission to a Ph.D. music program in the United States finally brought a closure to the spurious speculations. Joy later confirmed that the red herring emanated from her neck of the woods. The whistleblowers were her former boss and colleagues at NBC. The conspirators wanted Bankole to be the one to flush Joy out of UNILAG, but Bankole refused; may his soul rest in peace.[10]

---

9   Akin Euba's tenure at the University of Lagos was very short. He resigned in 1980.

10   Ayo Bankole too was at the University of Lagos for a short period—1969 to 1976. His tenure was truncated by a gruesome and gory incident. Bankole and his wife Toro were both brutally murdered while sleeping in their own house by his half brother in 1976.

Joy Nwosu and Her Church Choir at the University of Lagos, 1978.

**Joy Nwosu Receives a Farewell Gift from Her Church Choir
Members at the University of Lagos, 1978.**

Musical Training in the United States

In her quest to make a profound contribution to the music of her own ethnic group, Joy did an extensive research on Igbo folk tales before she left Nigeria for Michigan State University. She intended to write her dissertation on the importance of folk tales and folk songs in music education. Sadly enough, when she arrived in Michigan, out of exhilaration, Joy discussed her research proposal with another fellow student, a Ghanaian, who was already there before her, and had been struggling to get his prospectus approved. He secretly stole the idea from Joy and used it to write his own dissertation. Joy had to go back to the drawing board and started looking for a new topic. Her intent was to embark on a research that would be relevant to her culture. Again, she resorted to prayer, seeking the face of God for an inspirational theme.

As soon as Joy started praying, the Lord directed her to the huge book by Hornbostel-Sachs on classification of musical instruments. Coincidentally, at that time, Joy was taking courses in ethnomusicology that familiarized her with the works of these two ethnomusicologists. Joy took a closer look on their work on African instruments, and discovered that all African instruments were classified as idiophones. Joy disputed the logic of lumping together of instruments from the so-called developing world. But she could not attack Sachs and Hornbostel, giants in world music. Joy rather decided to research how her culture, the Igbo ethnic group, classifies musical instruments; it was an eye opening experience for Joy.

The Lord gave Joy everything she wrote in her dissertation through divine inspiration and hard work. Joy admits that it could not have come from her; certainly, it must have been a supernatural intervention. The findings were so bombastic that Joy had to change the chair of her doctoral committee, before she could continue with her dissertation. The title of Joy's dissertation was "A Preliminary Study of the Classification, Tuning and Educational Implications of the Standardization of Musical Instruments in Africa: The Nigerian Case."[11]

---

11   Joy Nwosu Lo-Bamijoko, "A Preliminary Study of the Classification, Tuning and Educational Implications of the Standardization of Musical Instruments in Africa: The Nigerian Case" (Ph.D. Dissertation, University of Michigan—Ann Arbor, 1981).

Joy Nwosu after a Voice Recital at Michigan State University, Ann Arbor, 1979.

Grotesque Welcome

As soon as Joy returned to Nigeria in 1982, she lifted the entire classification chapter of her dissertation and published it in the *Nigeria Magazine*. Out of elation for her gutsy accomplishment, Joy went on to share her impeccable research findings with her colleagues at UNILAG. Of course, it did not go well with Ekwueme in particular. He simply dwarfed the publication and informed her that *Nigeria Magazine* was not a scholarly magazine. That same year, *African Music Magazine* heard of Joy's article, requested for it, and published a reprint of the essay.

On her return to Nigeria from Michigan State, Joy was looking forward to a more cordial and peaceful atmosphere at her job. Her credential wahala[12] had been put to rest; so she thought. Joy was also hoping that advancement in her job was a slam-dunk now that she has earned her Ph.D. Unknown to Joy at the time was the fact that she was a woman trying to foray into the turf where only men flourished in Nigeria, a patriarchic society—indeed, a man's world. Her induction into the volatile pantheon of music dons was an up-hill battle smeared with public scandal and controversy. The male dominated academic coterie lampooned Joy's doctorate degree. Joy narrates the insidious, dehumanizing, denigrating, and humiliating reception given to her by her male contemporaries, even outside of the music circle:

> When I returned to Nigeria in January, 1982, the news went round that I was back. Some people were happy for me, especially my family, but others had mixed feelings. The disputants argued that I could never have completed a Ph.D. program in three years; that I must have bought my Ph.D. degree from one of the American "diploma mills," that is, schools they heard sold diplomas to anyone who can afford them. A dramatist, whom I thought was my friend, travelled to the United States around that time, with a promise that he was going to use the opportunity to unmask my fraud. In fact, many of my other

---

12   Wahala = Trouble

colleagues were rooting for him and supporting his baseless quest. Late Samuel Akpabot, was well known for writing a column on *Sunday Times*[13] at that time, and I liked reading his column. One Sunday, his column was all about me. The preceding Sunday, he wrote about Nigerian female musicians, and I was not even mentioned. Then the next Sunday, the article was all about me. I was glad and believed that he was giving me a special treatment, and it was a "special treatment" indeed. Akpabot started with how I came back to Nigeria with a spurious Ph.D. diploma from an unknown and non-existent United States institution, and that I was parading about with fake credentials expecting the real musicians to respect me. I jolted off my seat! I was not expecting anything like that at all. I adjusted myself on my seat and tried to read again, and it was all there. He promised that very soon the truth about what I did in the United States will come out. He was referring to the man who went to the United States promising to unmask me. Akpabot went as far to mention some ladies that he thought sang better than me. These were women with less training and less qualification than me. In the end, he warned me about what he said he knew I did, and asked me to vacate UNILAG before I will be disgraced out of the place. After reading his extensive commentary about me, with no single positive statement, attributed to me musically, all I did was pray. I prayed and asked God to show me what to do, how to react, and how to respond to this man. Three days of serious praying and seeking God's face gave me an epiphany. I decided to debunk Akpabot's erratum with my own rebuttal. The Lord gave me one of my finest writings, and I went to the *Daily Times* office and handed the article personally to the *Sunday Times* editor. I told the editor that that was my response to what Akpabot wrote about me the previous Sunday, and that I wanted him to publish my rebuttal the very next Sunday. He did, and to make the story more juicy; it was published on Akpabot's own column. My ingenious response indeed brought a closure to all the frivolous

13   *Sunday Times* is one of the leading national newspapers in Nigeria. Its weekly publication is called the *Daily Times*.

speculations about my American credentials and I was finally exonerated from their nefarious plot. The man who went to the United States returned and also confirmed everything I wrote in my article. The next time Akpabot and I met at a conference, he doffed his hat to me.

From Mentor to Tormentor

In spite of the bickering and conniving to tarnish her reputation, Joy continued to perform with the Laz Ekwueme National Chorale. She later took time off to set up her own band and thereby establish her reputation at the national level as a performing superstar. Her involvement with the chorale dissipated as her schedule with her own band spiked. Joy also created a children's choir that kept her even more busy to the extent that she stopped singing with the Laz Ekwueme Chorale. One day, out of frustration, after the chorale's performance without Joy at an embassy, Ekwueme went to Joy's office, fuming, screaming, with steam shooting off his ears. He kicked the door to her office open and pointed his dreadful fingers at Joy. Ekwueme warned Joy sternly with an irascible voice, that she should consider herself swimming in dangerous water if she should ever miss any of his concerts again. It was at this point that Joy resolved to quit his choir for good.

In order to intimidate and scare the hell out of Joy, Ekwueme developed the habit of not knocking at her office door, but kicking it open with his foot anytime he wanted to talk to her about his choir. Once, he told Joy that she should know that the right hand must wash the left hand for peace to reign. Joy reminded him that when she returned from Michigan to do her fieldwork in Nigeria, she almost jeopardized her research because he insisted that she must travel with his choir to Ghana and to different states of Nigeria. Joy pleaded with Ekwueme to allow her some time to develop her own credits so that she can be promoted. At the utterance of these words, Ekwueme revealed the secret of how to get promotion in his 'own academic citadel.' Ekwueme told Joy that he decides who gets promoted or not promoted, and that it does not depend on how much credits she could accumulate, but on how well she serve him. Joy was mortified at such an egotistical utterance.

Victorious Promotion

From that day, Joy completely severed relationship with Ekwueme, minded her own business, and worked hard to write and get published. In 1985, when Joy thought she was ready to present herself for promotion, she sent in her application, and copies of her work. When Ekwueme received Joy's dossier, he considered it 'Dead on Arrival.' He laughed sarcastically at Joy and responded with a very denigrating memo in which he dwarfed all her work, and he personally went on to show Joy a copy of his evaluation. As he was walking away, he turns to Joy and said, "Unless you do as you are told, you should forget to ever be promoted in this university." Joy read his memo, went home and prayed. Joy placed the memo on her Bible and asked God to show her how to respond to it. The next morning, Joy was inspired to write a rebuttal that was so powerful that the then Dean of the Faculty of Arts decided to take up her case. He did, and got Joy promoted to Senior Lecturer in Music on 1 October, 1985. God bless Prof. Ashiwaju. With this triumphant elevation, Joy thought she was beginning to see the light at the end of the tunnel; but she was dead wrong. For the contentious promotion to Senior Lecturer in Music further escalated the strained relationship between the two titans—the battle ground was drawn between Joy and her mentor, Ekwueme, who has now transformed himself into a tormentor. Ekwueme used every ounce of his authority to thrust deadly blows into Joy's matters, to frustrate and impede her progress at UNILAG.

The morning after the news of Joy's promotion hit the campus; Ekwueme remained defiant with his atrocious tirades. He went to her office in his usual barbaric manner; kicked at her door in a loud bang, while wearing a wicked smile on his face, Ekwueme threatened Joy, "it will never happen again!" and it never did. By telling her that "it will never happen again," he meant he will never allow Joy to get promoted again; and he kept his word. Joy never received another promotion at UNILAG while Ekwueme was there as a Professor of Music. He blatantly blocked all her chances and avenues to move up in academic rank.

Joy Nwosu at the University of Lagos, 1985.

Joy Nwosu in Front of the Arts Block at the University of Lagos, 1985.

Promotion Logjam

Several years later, when Joy applied for Associate Professorship, Ekwueme convinced the new Vice Chancellor of the university, the late Prof. Adesola, to back him up. Rather than resolve the impasse, the Vice Chancellor decided to team-up with Ekwueme to forestall Joy's progress. In spite of the rapport between the two men, Joy still went on to complain to Adesola about Ekwueme's antics. Adesola simply told her to go and do whatever Ekwueme wanted her to do, and that she should stop being assertive. Adesola made it clear to Joy that he did not like assertive women. He closed with a popular Nigerian male chauvinistic and egotistic phrase, "I have four like you in my house." By this he meant he had four wives. To Joy, that was the last straw. Seeing no end in site with the stalemate, Joy decided to leave. There was no one else to turn to for support or counsel. Evidently, nobody was willing to take up her case and fight for her at UNILAG. At this point, Joy perceived her case to be a lost battle. She could not confide in any one in that institution.

Prevailing Prayer

Joy applied for a study leave, that was already overdue; but Adesola declined to approve it. As a devout Christian who was well experienced in spiritual warfare, Joy knew that the only way out was to consult the highest Authority, God, the creator of the whole universe, with whom, ALL THINGS ARE POSSIBLE. In desperation, Joy went on her knees to pray to God to help her. Her prayer was instantly answered with a glimmer of hope.

Shortly after this incident, a colleague showed up in Joy's office one morning to inform her that Adesola had embarked on a tour of Europe and America. Joy quickly ran to the deputy Vice Chancellor and told him that Adesola did not sign her papers before he left. The deputy peruses her letter and said, "You are asking for three years, that is why he declined your request. If you ask for one year at a time, I will sign it for you." Joy scurried to her office, personally retyped the letter, hurried back to the deputy, and he signed it for her. Joy left Nigeria the very next day for the United States in 1996. One month after her escape, Joy received a despondent letter in which Adesola furiously ordered her back, and threatened her with dismissal if she did not return to Nigeria. Joy sent him medical reports of her deteriorating health to let him know that even if she wanted, she could not return.

Joy later learned that Adesola took her case to the Appointments and Promotions Committee, and tried to get her fired. Some colleagues, who knew Joy and saw her name on the list of those to be dismissed, attended the committee meeting to find out what her crime was. Not satisfied with Adesola's excuses, the committee dismissed the case, thereby, helping Joy to keep her job while she was still in the United States. After spending the three years that the regulation permitted her in the United States, Joy returned to UNILAG in 1999 with the plan of spending a year to tidy up things and retire. But Adesola blatantly refused to give her back her job. With such a doleful cloud hanging over her job, the only option left was for Joy to tender her retirement papers and left for good. She was allowed to retire three years later, after Adesola was disgraced out of UNILAG. Adesola died shortly after this incident.

Ekwueme's Discomfiture

While all these fiasco was going on, the authorities at the helm of the university were surreptitiously plotting an ignominious debacle—the dissolution of the Department of Music created by Ekwueme. The authorities had a clear knowledge of Ekwueme's pathological destructive behaviors and they could see that the music department was not making progress neither was it producing musicians. In other words, the purpose of establishing a music program in the university was nonexistent. The department was inept. When the authorities finally succeeded in facing out the music department, Joy decided to flee the country for good and immigrated to the United States.

Ekwueme could have done great things for music in Nigeria if only he had believed in people. He did not believe that anyone else could be referred to as a Professor of Music in Nigeria while he had that title. Ekwueme used to pompously brag to young amateur musicians in his choir that nobody will ever be called a Professor of Music in Nigeria while he is still alive. He would take these young guys to a room in his house and showed them a long pile of files containing curriculum vitae of other music faculties from all over Nigeria; files awaiting his evaluation and recommendation to professorship. Accordingly, Ekwueme was the only music professor in Nigeria for over two decades until his retirement in the early 2000s. He was so full of himself, arrogant, ego driven, and short sighted, because today, there are more than one Professor of Music in Nigeria; these were people Ekwueme had callously blocked from becoming professors for so many years while he was still in the academia. The University of Lagos authorities had to decimate Ekwueme's "golden egg" in order to flush him out of the system. What a shameful way to exit the academic career after serving for almost three decades. All Ekwueme[14] was after was to destroy and put down every trained musician in Nigeria, and subject them to stoop to him, thereby worship him as their "master." During Ekwueme's hay days, all the music lecturers in Nigeria were at his mercy. They could not advance to any level of professorship without his blessing. I label this ostentatious behavior as "academic witchcraft."

Recently, one of Joy's former students, who now reside in the United States, drove all the way from Philadelphia to attend her birthday celebrations. Her first question to Joy was, "Ma, why did you leave? We all needed you and you left." Joy gave her a simple answer. Joy departed because there was nothing else left for her to do. The music department was scrapped and the faculty became redundant. Her colleagues, some younger than her, were dead, if she had stayed, she does not know what would have become of her.

---

14 Lazarus Ekwueme has retired from the University of Lagos in the early 2000s. He is presently a traditional ruler in his home town in southeast region of Nigeria.

A Man of Honor and Integrity

In spite of all the evil intents of some of Joy's colleagues against her, God always infiltrate the camp of the enemy with some few righteous ones to counter the assault of the kingdom of darkness. Joy relishes the support, counsel, and candor she received from Prof. Ade Ajayi. At this juncture, Joy eulogizes this extremely compassionate man. Ajayi attended all the concerts Joy did at UNILAG. He and his beautiful wife would sit right at the front row where Joy could see them. When Joy started performing at the Christopher Oyesiku epic concerts at the University of Ibadan, they were there too. Ajayi was the one who sent Joy off to Michigan to pursue her Ph.D. He was the third person she showed her letter of admission and he was extremely happy for her that within a month of her getting that letter, Joy was off to Michigan. As a result of Ajayi's support, Joy did not experience any administrative bottle-neck, that is, impediment.

It was Ajayi who made it possible for many university academic staff to have a roof over their heads when they retire from service. It all began when Prof. Chike Obi, the eminent mathematician, retired, and did not have a house of his own. At that time, the annual salary of a professor was a little over two thousand US dollars. In the light of such meager wages, Obi could not build a house of his own on such a pittance. That was why when lecturers were hired they were given free accommodation and a car loan to alleviate the pain of their poverty salary. However, in the true sense of it, this only gives a false sense of well being. Obi stayed at his free accommodation house on campus for several years after his retirement as the university looked for ways to help him. Obi's experience became an eye opener for all faculty members at the university, for it could happen to any of them to find oneself on the streets after retirement. Joy cannot explain how it happened, or what he did, but Ajayi was able to persuade the Lagos State government to allocate land to UNILAG for distribution to any academic staff who had been teaching for ten years or more.

The first batch of land went to the professors, and as would be expected, they were all men—another definitive manifestation of a patriarchic enclave. As the adage goes, "hell hath no fury like a woman scorned." Accordingly, by the time the second batch was released, the women of the university had formed their own branch of the University Women Association, and they were out in arms demanding their right as faculty members of the university in the allocation of plots of land. They got it! The second batch of land was shared among all members of the faculty who qualified without discrimination; Joy was one of the lucky recipients who got a piece of the cake. Today, when Joy goes to Nigeria, she knows she has a place she could call her own home; all thanks to Ajayi who had the foresight to fight and win such a battle for his colleagues. Joy is aware that this program is still going on today, and that the University of Lagos is likely the first and only university in Nigeria that has done this, and that good gesture is still in motion today.

Joy Nwosu's House in Lagos.

Professional Career in Nigeria—Phase Two

The professional activities of Joy in Nigeria included teaching, song recitals, full stage performances, choral conducting, radio and television broadcasting, radio and television performances, concert tours, and skits. Joy also attended national and international conferences as well as workshops. Joy was chair of the music department at the University of Lagos from 1986 to 1987, and was later chair of the Music Unit of the Centre for Cultural Studies, University of Lagos, from 1989 to 1992. As a music faculty at UNILAG, Joy taught several courses including voice, beginning piano, fundamentals for music literacy, African music, choral repertoire, stage production, and dance. She enjoyed teaching voice the most, since that was her primary instrument. During her tenure, Joy was the only female lecturer in the Department of Music; hence, it was not surprising that she had mostly female students. Joy finally retired from the Centre for Cultural Studies, University of Lagos, as a Senior Research Fellow on 1 November, 1999. Joy held several academic and administrative positions in Nigeria and all around the globe. Some of the most prominent positions are listed below:

Academic and Administrative Positions

1. 1952 Elementary School Teacher, C.M.S. School, Ogwi, Enugu, Nigeria.
2. 1962 Instructor, Holy Rosary College, Enugu, Nigeria.
3. 1975 Music Lecturer, Department of Music, University of Lagos, Nigeria.
4. 1985 Senior Lecturer in Music, University of Lagos, Nigeria.
5. 1986 - 1987 Acting Chair, Department of Music, University of Lagos, Nigeria.
6. 1988 - 1997 Senior Research Fellow, Centre for Cultural Studies, University of Lagos, Nigeria.
7. 1989 - 1992 Chair, Music Unit, Centre for Cultural Studies, University of Lagos, Nigeria.

Other Professional Experience

1. 1965 - 1967 Translator, English/Italian, Nigerian Embassy, Rome, Italy.
2. 1967 - 1968 Translator, English/Italian, UNITELE FILM—A film Company, Rome, Italy.
3. 1968 - 1969 Translator, English/Italian, Ghana Embassy, Rome, Italy.
4. 1970 – 1972 Welfare Officer, International Red Cross, Bowaki, Ivory Coast.
5. 1972 - 1975 Producer, Music Programs, Nigerian Broadcasting Corporation, Lagos, Nigeria.
6. 1977 Assistant Director, Music Programs, World Festival of the Black Arts and Culture (FESTAC), Lagos, Nigeria.
7. 1986 - 1988 Chairwoman, Anambra State Council for Arts and Culture, Enugu, Nigeria.
8. 1982 - 1996 Organist and Choir Director, Chapel of Christ Our Light, University of Lagos Catholic Community, Lagos, Nigeria.
9. 1986 - 1992 Music and Choir Director, Junior Choir, Shepherd Hill Baptist Church, Lagos, Nigeria.
10. 1991 - 1994 Nigerian Representative, Commonwealth Music Association, Lagos, Nigeria.
11. 1994 - 1996 General Secretary, Commonwealth Music Association, worldwide.
12. 1997 - 2000 Vocal Music Teacher, K-8, Patterson Public Schools, New Jersey, United States.
13. 2000 – 2008 Vocal Music Teacher, Irvington High School, New Jersey, United States.

Performances in Nigeria

Joy performed in so many stellar concerts that she cannot even recollect all of them. She sang at funerals, marriages, churches, socials, universities, embassies, hotels, and before the cream of Nigerian high profile society.

In a nutshell, Joy accepted invitations anywhere she could find a receptive audience. Joy did all of these hoping that more Nigerians will develop a taste for *Bel Canto*. In spite of the fact that she was doing these to encourage and develop talents in Nigeria, there were some appalling moments that nearly crippled the cause she was promoting.

Joy once received an invitation to perform at a funeral at the renowned Cathedral Church of Christ, Lagos. While she was singing, and her voice was soaring and filling the nave of the church; she noticed the officiating pastor bent down and did something. Immediately the microphone went off while she was still singing. Joy turned slowly to look at him and pointed to the microphone to let him know that it was off. Instead, she noticed a smack on his face, as if to dare her to sing without a microphone. The pastor did not know who he was messing with. Joy belted, switched on her inner microphone, and went on with her song and finished it with a flare and glamour. Joy turned slowly to catch a glimpse of the priest after her brilliant performance; she caught him looking at her in disbelief, or as the British would say, he was gobsmacked. That was when she understood the conspiracy; the pastor's intent was to ground her performance, for what reason, she did not know.

At another occasion, Joy and Richard Bucknor—piano accompanist, were invited to perform at the twenty-fifth wedding anniversary of an old school mate. The ceremony took place at a village church somewhere in the then Eastern Nigeria. They performed the "Panis Angelicus" by Cesar Franck. At the end of the performance, Bucknor and Joy quickly left the church, but before they could sneak out, they heard someone called out after them, "excuse me; excuse me." They turned and there was Chief Jerome Udoji, the famous Udoji of the Udoji commission.[15]

---

15 Chief Jerome Udoji's high point of service was when, from 1972 to 1974, he served as the chairman of the Nigerian Public Service Review Commission, popularly known as the "Udoji Commission." The commission awarded the civil servants—government workers, of the time in Nigeria a fantastic wage increase and bonuses that spontaneously sent virtually all the recipients on shopping sprees.

She knew him very well. He had attended her concerts, but she was surprised to see him at the village. "It's you Joy!" he said, "I thought I was discovering a new voice in my village." "So you are from here Sir?" Joy replied. "That was my nephew you sang for. You are just as exquisite as always." He added, and they parted.

Joy Nwosu and Richard Bucknor, 1987.

There was a time Joy mounted a colossal concert at UNILAG Main Auditorium. Before the show began, she asked the video technician to record the program for her. He did, and after the show, the technician gave her a CD of the concert. The then director of the Center for Cultural Studies at UNILAG asked if he could see the recording because he was not able to attend. Joy was happy to oblige, thinking that he had a good intention towards her; sadly enough, she was wrong, because that was the end of that CD. Joy never saw it again. This pernicious experience had a sense of déjà vu about it. Has Joy not encountered this before? Oh yes! It was the program she did with Art Alade at the Nigerian Television Authority in Lagos. This simply made Joy to start thinking that there was a concerted effort by some of her colleagues to extirpate all evidence of her performances and sagacity.

These dastardly behaviors, merely confirm the envy, jealousy, rancor, and rivalry that are so rampant among artists in Nigeria. Such despicable attitudes do not encourage growth, creativity, and inventiveness. Rather, these clandestine maneuvers are eating up every fabric of artistic and intellectual purview in Nigeria, thereby, creating regression, that is best described as the "African Tango"—one step forward today, immediately sequel by two steps backward the following day. This type of nemesis has suffocated budding artists over the years. Many had given up and beaten hands down in the course of the fracas, while some few lucky ones, such as me, immigrated to Europe and the United States to develop their talents, acquire thorough training, and flourish globally; far away from their native country where talents are constantly subverted. That is why, I have never gone back to Nigeria since I immigrated to the United States in 1994, and I do not plan to go back any time soon.

Suffice it to say, all the Nigerian composers, pianists, organists, and musicologists with international reputation were trained mainly in Europe and the United States. None were locally trained in Nigeria. You may ask, why? The answer is so glaring. If they had stayed in Nigeria, they would be destroyed while still in incubation by those who suppose to encourage and help them to develop their God-given gifts in music. Unfortunately, the most talented ones who could not escape such deleterious conflicts blatantly shy away from graduate music schools in Nigeria. They are patiently awaiting opportunities to gain admission to pursue a Master's or Ph.D. programs in Europe or the United States. These wise youngsters have vowed never to attempt the graduate programs in Nigeria. They know they would receive proper training, encouragement, love, support, protection, and ultimately, earn higher degrees from foreign professors. These guys do not care if it will take them ten years or a whole life time to get the opportunity they are seeking outside of Nigeria.

Emancipation of Nigerian Women

Joy programmed over fifty outstanding concerts and recitals of solo and group performances in Nigeria and abroad. In Nigeria, she performed in Lagos, Ibadan, Benin City, Enugu, Port Harcourt, Owerri, and Nsukka. Her international appearances include Legon and Accra in Ghana, Dublin, London, Rome, and the United States. She also did Command Performances for the Hungarian and Mauritian Heads of States. A progenitor in her own right, Joy was one of the few female musicians who opened the floodgates of opportunities to other female musicians in Nigeria. Prior to her era, the music industry in Nigeria was exclusively dominated by men, either in art music, traditional or popular music. It was a man's world and men took full control and advantage of the opportunity. Following her ingenuity, other female musicians, especially in the popular music arena, emulated Joy and formed their own bands, started performing publicly, and released LPs, CDs, and music videos. Joy's novelty, embolden the women that they too can be part of what they thought was alien to them. In other words, Joy gave the Nigerian women a voice to speak and make meaningful contribution to the music landscapes in Nigeria. Accordingly, the name, Joy Nwosu, signifies her proclivity toward the emancipation of Nigerian women and individualistic empowerment. Today, Nigerian female musicians could celebrate and see Joy as a role model, hero, warrior, and mentor. That is why it was not surprising that Joy had to pay a steep price for her sagacity and trailblazing efforts, for having the effrontery to venture into, and compete with men in the field that they thought solely belongs to them in Nigeria.

Mammoth Music Production

Following the completion of her doctoral studies in the United States, Joy formed her own fifteen-piece band and called it, "Joy Nwosu and Her Ensemble." In all, the band gave three concerts, one of which was tagged, "The Nigerian Scene." There was a revolutionary song frequently performed by the band titled, "The Call." The song decries the fate of women in Nigeria. It says: "I am a woman and I am angry. I am angry because I am a woman. You have to be a woman to know why I am angry."[16]

In 1985, the Federal Directorate of Culture and Archives, as part of its program geared towards encouraging and enhancing the Nigerian artists, co-sponsored the production of Joy's Marathon Silver Jubilee Independence Concert at the National Theatre Main Auditorium, on 26 October, 1985. The epic concert, initiated by Joy as her contribution to the celebration of the Silver Jubilee Independence of Nigeria, consisted of three separate performances each day. The first part was classical music. Selections were drawn from popular art songs by Nigerian and Western composers, as well as from operatic repertoires. The performances were in full costumes, demarcated with an hour break after the first part. The second part featured popular songs from 1960 to 1985—an historical survey of popular music in Nigeria since independence, performed instrumentally by Joy's band while she changes costumes backstage or during intermissions. The third part show case folk songs written by Joy. Some of her most beautiful and thought provoking songs were heard by the end of the day. Below is a synopsis of some of Joy's stellar performances in Nigeria:

1. 1975 - 1976 Nigerian Broadcasting Corporation Cultural Nights.
2. 1977 World Festival of Black Arts and Culture—FESTAC, Star Performer.

---

16   Gladys Akatakpo, "Joy Nwosu: People's Taste for Music," *Lagos Life*, Thursday, 23 April and Wed, 29 April, 1987.

3. 1978 Show Unlimited, National Theatre.
4. 1982 Christmas Carols, NTA Lagos, National Theatre, and UNILAG[17] Auditorium.
5. 1983 Music Lessons, Nigerian Television Authority—NTA, Lagos.
6. 1985 - 1988 Marathon Show: A Six Hour non stop show, National Theatre.
7. 1991 Convocation Musical, UNILAG Auditorium.
8. 1991 and 1993, *Creation* by Haydn. She was Angel Gabriel, MUSON Centre.[18]
9. 1992 and 1993, *Messiah* by Handel—Soprano, UNILAG Auditorium.
10. 1972 - 1993 Performed on Enugu Radio and TV, Ibadan TV, and Lagos Radio and TV.

Joy also performed in several Hotels, such as The Eko Holiday Inn, Sheraton Hotel Banquet Hall, Federal Palace Hotel, and so many other places. Joy has a very long list of classical solo repertoire that she had sung over the decades, but her favourites include:

Climb Every Mountain, Richard Rodgers.
Loveliest of Trees, John Duke.
I Can't Be Talking of Love, John Duke.
The Lord's Prayer, Albert Hay Mallotte.
Bless This House, Carl Strommen.
Orpheus with His Lute, William Schuman.
Ah! Mio Cor, George Frederic Handel.
O del mio dolce ardor, Christoph Gluck.
Per la gloria d'adorarvi, G.B. Bononcini.
An die Musik, Franz Schubert.

---

17   UNILAG = University of Lagos, Nigeria.
18   MUSON = Musical Society of Nigeria, Lagos.

Die manner sind mechant! An meinem Herzen, Robert Schumann.
Autumn Thoughts, Edvard Grieg.
Tu che di gel sei cinta, Giacomo Puccini.
Poeme d'un Jour, Gabriel Faure.
Recontre Toujours Adieu, Gabriel Faure.

Career in the United States

Joy immigrated to the United States in 1996 where, for two years, she taught vocal music at Paterson Public Schools, and for eight years she taught vocal music and directed three choral groups: Concert Choir, Festival Choir, and Gospel Choir, at Irvington High School, New Jersey. She won several trophies and accolades with her beautiful Festival Choir at various choral competitions in the United States. However, life in the United States was not rosy at first, but in the end, the good Lord gave her victory over several daunting situations.

Due to the political upheavals and incessant conflicts within the academia in Nigeria, Joy was completely burnt out all through her final year at the University of Lagos. She could no longer function mentally. Joy experienced an intellectual block. By the time she arrived in the United States in 1996, Joy was completely inundated, drained, and empty—physically, spiritually, and emotionally. Joy spent a whole year under her daughter's care to recuperate from the trauma she had incurred at UNILAG. After one year of staying at home doing nothing, Joy began to itch to go out and find a job. The only job Joy knew how to do very well was teaching music. Thus, Joy sent out applications for a teaching position at various universities all over the United States—five hundred applications in all. She heard from all the institutions with high praise of her experience and accomplishments, but no job offer. Joy was afraid to try public schools. The first public school she taught after graduating from Michigan State University left her with the dread of high schools. It was in Philadelphia, and before she could assume teaching, a teacher in the same school was shot dead by a student.

Rather than teach in a public school, Joy decided to take a crash course in Home Aid. She worked in homes, cleaning, cooking, and caring for the home bound sick for two years. One day, after completing a difficult chore in the home of a very big bed bound lady, Joy cried in the rain on her way home, asking God, "Is this what you have brought me to do in America with a Ph.D.?" God answers prayers, all the time, in His own way and at His own time. Joy's tear-filled-prayer was expedited to the presence of the Lord by the ministering angels—angels are indeed on assignment. Her agency called Joy later that day to inform her that she should not go back to that home. The next day, Joy was reassigned to another home, supposedly with lighter duties. The lady in this new home had a grandson who was designated to move his grandmother with Joy any time she needed to be moved. They worked well for only one week before the lady and her grandson planned a scheme that would have cost Joy's agency a lot of money if they had succeeded.

Joy arrived for work one morning and the grandson, who by the way was wearing a monitoring gadget on his ankle, told Joy that he had to see his case worker that morning. Joy told him to wait for her to get someone else to help her before he could leave. He declined and left. Joy called her agency, told them what had happened and asked for someone to be sent immediately to assist her. The agency called the case worker of the boy and found out that he had no appointment that morning. While they were looking for him to get him back to the house, his grandmother started to fret, and told Joy that she must be moved to ease herself. Joy told her that she should wait for someone to come and help her to move. The woman knew very well that Joy was not supposed to move her alone, but she cried and fussed. Joy tried other options that would allow her to do it on the bed without soiling the bed, but the woman refused. In the end, Joy had to move her alone.

Moving this woman to the commode was easy because the commode was very close to the bed. Joy moved her so fast from the bed to the commode that she did not know how it happened. When she was done, Joy asked her to sit and wait until she could get assistance to move her back to the bed. At this point, the woman started wailing, cursing, and throwing tantrums. In the end, Joy had to succumb to her tirade and moved the woman again back to the bed all by herself. This time, the woman dropped her whole weight on Joy, expecting her to drop her. Joy mustered all her energy, held on and dropped her on the bed; at the same time, Joy heard a click on her back. Joy had broken her back bone. Joy called her agency to report what had happened. The case worker showed-up, while her agency sent a car to remove Joy from the house and take her to the agency's doctor. It took Joy three months of therapy and eventually, an operation on her spinal cord, before she could recuperate to use her left leg. After that incident, her qualms about teaching in the public school system disintegrate. God had His way. The accident shot the door to the condescending blue collar job and ultimately paved the trajectory to what she loved doing most—teaching.

Paterson Public Schools

As soon as Joy was well enough to work, she applied and got a teaching job with the Paterson School Board as a vocal music teacher. Joy immediately registered for the Alternate Teachers Certification courses at the William Patterson University, for her teachers' certification. Fortunately for Joy, the training ran parallel with her new job. This way, she was able to teach, earn money, and study concurrently. At the completion of the course, Joy was among the few selected teachers awarded the Dodge Fellowship.[19]

At Paterson, Joy taught in two schools, traveling from one school to the other, and also moving from class to class within each school. She had no official classroom of her own or personal office to plan and prepare lessons. Joy worked from a cart. She had wonderful students who looked forward every morning to their music class. Joy chose songs from different popular categories—the movies, songs by popular artists,

---

19   The Dodge Fellowship Awards are funded by the Geraldine R. Dodge Foundation to encourage and recognize outstanding new teachers as they enter the teaching profession through New Jersey's alternative licensure program.

songs written specially for school choruses, even songs brought in by the students themselves. Her time was only forty minutes for each class. At the beginning of every school year, Joy would give her students a pep talk about what her class was about. She would give them the syllabus, and let them know how she would run and grade her class for the year. Joy tells anyone who was in her class by mistake, that he or she was free to leave, and some would leave. Not all of them liked to take music tests. Some of the students thought music was an easy way to get a grade, but when they heard that they would take written and practical tests, they dropped the class.

Joy divided her forty minutes by doing breathing and vocal exercises for the first ten minutes. This was followed by basic fundamentals, one music concept at a time, for another ten minutes. Finally, they would sing the song for the day by first drawing a contour of the song on the score. Joy always taught her songs by first using the Finale software to write out the basic melody of the song so that they could see how it contoured. Joy met with some of her students three times a week, and some twice a week. This approach enabled her to work on one song for a whole week, review the song quickly the following week, and go into another song. Before the end of the school year, each class would chose one song that they liked best, and prepare that song for an end of year school assembly. Joy had fun teaching and her students had fun learning from her. During her second year at Paterson, Joy won another fellowship, the Master Teacher Award given by the New Jersey Performing Arts Center (NJPAC), for music teachers in the New Jersey schools. To win this award, the contestants had to submit a lesson plan for teaching their area of music.

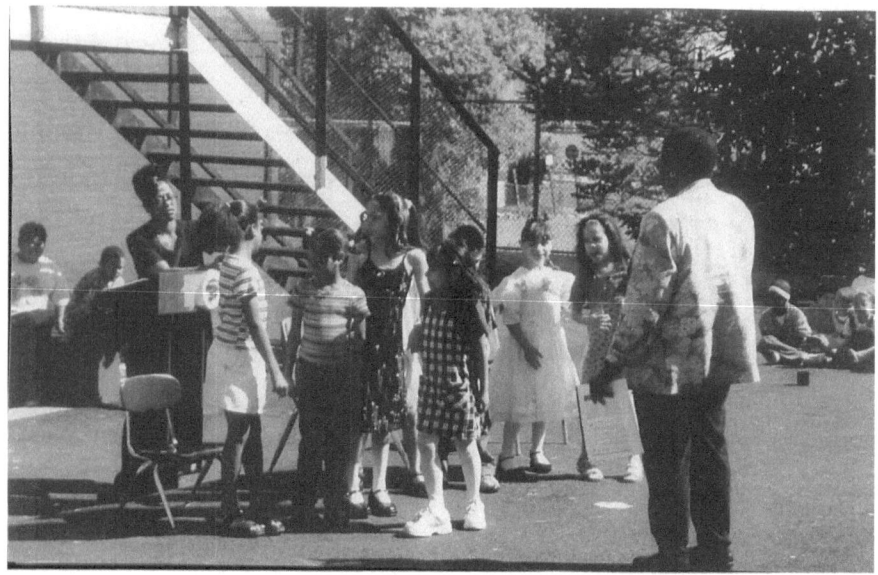

Joy Nwosu in the United States, 1999.

Irvington High School

After two years at Paterson schools, Joy was hired by the Irvington Public Schools to teach high school vocal music. She had her own official classroom at this high school which made her work a lot easier. Her aim at Irvington high school was to get her students to read from the score. It was not easy with only forty-five minutes of class time; hence, she inaugurated an after school choir. To motivate her choir to read music, Joy entered them for choral competitions, especially the one under the auspices of the American Choral Directors Association (ACDA). There was a reading section at the competition. At first, her principal assisted her to maintain the costs of the choir, but when the budget cuts was implemented, her choir was the first to go.

Three years before Joy finally retired; she had a crushing experience that truncated her long term goals at Irvington school. Every year, her choir always sang at the commencement of the school. That gloomy year, she had a new supervisor who was not appreciative of her performance style and teaching technique. Joy always conducted her choir with pre-recorded accompaniment. He wanted her to play the piano accompaniment and conduct at the same time; when Joy refused, explaining that her method had worked well for her, he decided to accompany the choir himself. Without rehearsing with the choir, not even once, he stationed himself at the piano on the day of the performance and threw the choir completely off. This debacle happened during a commencement ceremony! One could infer Joy's state of mind at such a catastrophic fiasco and public ridicule. Joy did not know whether he did it purposely or not, apparently, it was a woeful flop. Joy managed to salvage what was left of her presentation by going back to her pre-recorded accompaniment for the last song.

Joy Nwosu and Her Students at Irvington School, in Concert at the School Hall, 2005.

Joy Nwosu and Her Students at Irvington High School, in Concert, 2005.

The following day, at a post-concert session with her choir, her students came up with all kinds of reasons why this man derailed their concert. Joy could only see it as an attempt on his part to set her up for failure. She took full responsibility for that concert because she allowed him to impose his method on her; but as a supervisor, he should have known better not to interfere with a method that had worked so well for Joy.

The next school year, Joy's supervisor took a number of measures that ascertained Joy that he was setting her up. First, in order to stop her from giving concerts in the school, which she continued to do, he took the vocal music course from her, Joy's major area of specialization. Second, he pushed Joy out of the classroom, put her in a locker room, and assigned her piano to teach. Of course, having been trained to teach music, Joy was equipped to teach any course in the discipline, especially a course like piano, her minor area. Joy tackled that course in a way that no one had ever taught it before in that school. The man later admitted this claim! During her last concert at Irvington High, before he took the vocal music course from her, Joy saw him with the school's principal watching the concert, as he was busy critiquing the performance instead of letting the principal watch the show and form her own conclusions.

At the meeting of the district music teachers the following week, he described Joy's concert to her colleagues as the most anti-musical thing he had ever seen. That was the last straw for Joy. She went home that day, prayed and asked God in her usual manner to show her how to deal with the situation. God did; she got up in the middle of the night, and crafted a letter to her principal to report him for harassing her and trifling with her job in front of her colleagues. Joy put a copy of the letter into his mail box. Joy only copied him, she did not want the letter to get to the board, but she would have, if he had reacted differently. When he read his copy, he ran to Joy's classroom to deny ever trying to set her up. Joy used the opportunity of that letter also to clarify what happened at the graduation ceremony, and he understood where she was going with that.

After that incident, Joy began planning her retirement, and did retired two years later. This man's rants and malign of Joy's honorable service did not impede her from winning the Teacher of the Month Award at Irvington High School in 2007. Joy enjoyed teaching because she loved what she did. She tried to make it interesting for her students because that was the best way she could get them focused.

Joy is blessed with three wonderful children—Amanda Onwuka, Edochie Samuel Nwosu, and Hana Lo-Bamijoko. Her youngest daughter writes poems and lyrics to songs and she also sings beautifully. Joy is a hex-linguist,[20] fluent in French, Spanish, Italian, English, Igbo, and Yoruba Language.[21] For relaxation, Joy loves reading novels, and watching good movies on television. She enjoys traveling too, which she does a lot of these days, but in those days, she was extremely restricted because of her hectic academic schedule.

---

20 Hex-linguist = a person fluent in, understands or speaks six different languages.

21 The biography of Joy Nwosu Lo-Bamijoko is based on several personal interviews with her in the United States, between March 2006 and June 2011, including numerous formal and informal discussions, until this book went into production in fall 2011.

Joy Nwosu and Her Students at Irvington High School, New Jersey, to see a Broadway Show, "Phantom of the Opera," 2004.

Joy Nwosu at a Wedding in Onitsha, Nigeria, 2005.

Joy Nwosu with Family, 2005.

Music Scholarship

In the area of music scholarship, Joy is one of the pioneers of music education in Nigeria. Joy, Bankole, and Ekwueme, jointly founded the Department of Music at the University of Lagos. Joy presented several papers at conferences in Nigeria and abroad. Her area of interests in African ethnomusicology is wide. Joy has researched and published numerous articles on such topics as tuning systems, classification of Nigerian musical instruments, music education, Nigerian art music, popular music, performance practice, and the recording industry. A précis of Joy's scholarly work is presented in chapter three. Joy was the editor of three reputable journals: *Music in Nigeria,* a publication of the Commonwealth Music Association, Nigeria Chapter; *The Nigerian Music Directory,* a publication under the auspices of the Commonwealth Music Association, Nigeria Chapter; and *Journal of the Musicological Society of Nigeria.*

Joy Nwosu at a Conference at the University of Lagos, 1985.

Joy Nwosu at a Conference at the National Theater, Lagos, 1987.

Awards

1. 1961 Eastern Nigerian Government Scholarship to study Music in Rome. It was given for outstanding performances at the then Eastern Nigerian Festivals of Arts.
2. 1976 Federal Government of Nigerian Scholarship for studies in the United States—the scholarship was given for outstanding performances on Radio and Television in Nigeria.
3. 1977 Government of the United States grant as a Visiting Artist to the United States—this grant was given for outstanding performance during the World Black and African Festival of the Arts—FESTAC.
4. 1978 The University of Lagos grant for Study Leave to the United States.

Honorary Awards

1. 1980 University of Michigan dissertation grant, U.S.A.
2. 1991 The SOLIDRA Award, Nigeria.
3. 1993 The Commonwealth Foundation Fellowship Award, U.S.A.
4. 1998 Dodge Fellowship Award, U.S.A.
5. 2000 NJPAC Master Teacher Award at New Jersey, in the United States, U.S.A.

Chapter 2

It is a Man's World

In other to fully comprehend the ordeal that Joy Nwosu was subjected to by her male counterparts in Nigeria, it is imperative to give a brief statistical accounts of the disproportionate gap between men and women teaching music in Nigerian higher institutions. Up to her retirement from the University of Lagos in 1999, Joy was the only female lecturer in music at that institution. Presently, the situation has not changed at UNILAG. At the Department of Music, Obafemi Awolowo University, Ile-Ife, all the music lecturers are men. The music department at the College of Education, Ilesha, had only one female faculty until early 2000s. As of the time I left the shores of Nigeria in the mid-1990s, all the lecturers were men at the Department of Music, The Polytechnic at Ibadan. The premier music department at the University of Nigeria, Nsukka, is no exception. The department had only male lecturers until Joy left Nigeria in 1996. We do not know whether this tradition has changed. Not only in the academia. Joy affirms that every facet of the Nigerian life sidetracked women, and women had to work ten times as much as their male counterparts to step on to the turf regarded as the exclusive boundaries for men—a monolithic approach in a patriarchic society. Things are gradually changing today because of education for women. Illiteracy, that is largely the plight of women, especially women in northern Nigeria, is still the driving force behind the old tradition of mistreatment of women in the work force.

To demonstrate the plight of women in twenty-first century Nigeria, I have decided to quote extensively from Joy's new book, *Mirror of Our Lives,* to bolster these assertions. Below is a dialogue from *Mirror of Our Lives,* between two women, sharing from their own personal experiences, the realization and impact of a man's world as practiced among the Igbo ethnic group of southeast Nigeria:

"What will she tell people? That her marriage has failed, that she is a failure? What will they think? No one will believe that it is not her fault. It is always the woman's fault... She also knows that anything can happen in Nigeria. It is a man's world, and rules can be changed or twisted."[22]

"Among the Igbo, the man usually lorded over the females in the family, even his mother, because he was a man... But Miss Nelly was the only one who knew where the shoe hurts. Gab lived in Lagos with his family, Emeka in Awka with his family. She lived alone in Port Harcourt. As a single woman in a cosmopolitan city like Port Harcourt, she could not have a life. It was different when she had them. They were company. Now, if she went to a party alone, the men ogled her as soon as they saw that she was alone. An unaccompanied lady at a party was viewed as someone desperate for a man. She could not eat out alone. Only bad and loose women did that. If she tried to eat out alone, the first man to notice that she was alone tried to claim ownership of her or forced himself on her. She could not have a social life. Other women would think that she was after their husbands. She was a prisoner in the city. The only way she could be free to have a life was to marry; to answer to a name; to become a second, third, or fourth wife to a man; or to become an only wife to a widower; unfortunately, this widower had seven children... She married Colonel Imoh on a bright sunny day.

22   Joy Nwosu Lo-Bamijoko, *Mirror of Our Lives: Voices of Four Igbo Women* (Bloomington, IN: iUniverse Publishing, 2011), 47.

It was a Sunday wedding… She, on her part, married him to put an end to her family's dependence on her and to answer to a name. Her new name carried with it a lot of freedom, freedom to do a lot of those things she could not do as a single woman. She had someone now to cover her back. Even if the husband was not there, she had his name to protect her. The marriage was the first thing she had done for herself."[23]

"Remember, don't let what people claim is the norm stop you. That is where I think I failed. I let tradition stop me. Every time I wanted to move forward, I was reminded that I was a woman and that there were things a woman was not supposed or allowed to do. I was not supposed to buy myself a car. My father, husband, or sugar daddy should do that for me, and if by chance I had enough money to buy my car, I was to give the credit for buying the car to the man in my life. The same thing goes for buying a piece of land—that is an abomination. Or buying a house; unheard of. If you want to go out to a party, a social, a restaurant, anywhere you meet people, you must be accompanied. Or the story will go around that you are from a bad family, a desperate woman, or a whore. This makes you a prisoner in your own home."[24]

"Oh yes, Miss Nelly, I experienced that when I walked into a restaurant alone in Lagos," she says… "It was harrowing. I went for a job interview in Victoria Island, on a Monday. I was in a taxi when I sighted a restaurant that specializes in Italian food. I made a note to explore the place after my interview. Later that day, I retraced my steps back to this restaurant, entered, and hoped to socialize with someone who speaks Italian … the place was buzzing like a market when I stepped in, but as soon as I walked in, everything went dead quiet. I looked around and saw hefty white men, wearing only their undershirts, red in the face and skin, as red as roasted lobsters, at round tables. There were no black persons there. All of them, in unison, turned their back on me as I entered, and they started to eat and swear at me over their food. My instinct told me to turn around and leave, but my stubbornness stopped

---

23   (Lo-Bamijoko 2011, 75)
24   (Lo-Bamijoko 2011, 83)

me and reminded me that this was my country. I walked over to the bar to order something, and the barman walked away and went to the back of the bar into the kitchen. I heard these red-bodied men hiss and curse at me in Italian. One said, '*Che fa qui la putana?'* I was shocked to hear him call me a whore! They did not know that I could understand them. I waited for the barman to return, and when he did, he said in a very thick English accent, 'so, lady, why are you still here, eh? This is no place for you. Can't you see?' And then he swore at me, '*Mannagia caspita!'* and shook his hands at me in that unique Italian way, with his fingers held together… Damn me? I thought. I turned around, took a last and courageous look at the men and at the barman, and slowly walked out of the place." Miss Nelly turns sharply at her with a shocked look on her face. "That is the kind of danger you must avoid."[25]

The men she narrowly escaped were construction men who worked for G. Cappa Italian Construction Company based in Lagos, Nigeria, and that restaurant is their little Italy. "But Miss Nelly," she says, "if I had been accompanied, it would have been a different scene altogether." Miss Nelly nods in agreement. Continuing their conversation about being a woman in their community, she says, "Let's say that your father is enlightened and well-to-do, and he wants to educate all his children, males and females, but your family will expect you to pay back, and you can never, ever pay back enough. That is the story of my life."[26]

"But hold on"—Ify quickly interrupts her as she nods her head vigorously in agreement—"that is the price for educating an Igbo woman! My family did not send me abroad. I went abroad on scholarship. When I was given the scholarship, my brother was furious. He wanted to know why the scholarship was given to me, the woman, and not to him, the man. He wanted me to go back to the scholarship board and tell them that there was a man in the house and ask them to transfer my scholarship to him. I told him that if he wanted a scholarship, he should earn one. When I returned after ten years of sojourn abroad, my brother

25 (Lo-Bamijoko 2011, 84)
26 (Lo-Bamijoko 2011, 85)

greeted me with, 'so you have stubbornly gone and come back? I want you to know that you are now responsible for training all my children.' When I told him that he was dreaming, he put a curse on me. He told me that I would never marry or have children." Ify hears Miss Nelly take in a very sharp breath. She turns in time to see Miss Nelly shake her head and frown. "That is my own experience with brothers," she says with sadness in her eyes. For the first time, Ify is seeing her sad.[27]

Miss Nelly stands and walks to the window facing a two-carriage road in front of her house. Ify walks over too and stands next to her. They both watched some young boys at a game of football—soccer, in the narrow street. The boys play and run to the side when a car comes by. There are no sidewalks. "My child, I am happy that you and the other girls did better than we did," she says quietly. "You all have fought so well, and I am proud of you. You have not failed as we did. The sacrifice we made for you did not go in vain." "Do you call this sacrifice, Miss Nelly? I call it unacceptable!" She turns to her puzzled. "It is not right that women should sacrifice their lives for men." But she knows Miss Nelly fought her battle the best way she could, and at least she broke away from the sharks. "I could never make such a sacrifice. I don't think anyone should." But Miss Nelly continues to speak quietly. "I am happy that you have reaped the benefits of our sacrifice. To see you girls do well is a victory to us, to me."[28]

---

27   (Lo-Bamijoko 2011, 85)
28   (Lo-Bamijoko 2011, 86)

Chapter 3

Scholarly Contributions to Nigerian Music

Joy Nwosu contributed several articles on African ethnomusicology in reputable journals and chapters in books. This chapter presents a concise overview of selected five essays and a book that best represent the crux of her research on Nigerian music and culture.

Shortly after Joy completed her Ph.D. studies and returned to Nigeria, she published her first article, "Tuning Methods of African Musical Instruments: Some Examples from Nigeria and Ghana."[29] She opens this essay by pinpointing some of the factors that influence the tuning system of African musical instruments. These factors include material from which the instrument is made, the effect of the material on the sound quality of the instrument, and psychological factors such as reasons for choosing one texture or one quality of sound over another that might affect the pitch. For the specificity of this topic, Joy focuses the article on the non-physical factors of these methods and uses three musical instruments to illustrate her argument. These instruments are *ngedegwu* (xylophone), *ubo-aka* (thumb piano), and *oja* (three-

---

29 Joy Nwosu Lo-Bamijoko, "Tuning Methods of African Musical Instruments: Some Examples from Nigeria and Ghana," *Nigeria Magazine,* No. 142 (1982): 15-24.

note flute). In Nigeria, and specifically among the Igbo people, the classification of musical instruments takes two issues into consideration, the organological and anthropological factors; that is, the construction of the instrument and the effect of the culture on the instrument. Joy astutely classifies musical instruments among the Igbo into three categories: rhythmic, melodic, and rhythmo-melodic. All Nigerian instruments classified under *iku* have two features in common—they have fixed tones, and they are struck or beaten to produce sound. The tuning of instruments under *iku* aims at producing one distinct sound for each gong, slit drum lip, or xylophone slab.

In *ngedegwu,* the slabs are tuned by carving out the center to lower the pitch, and sharpening the edges to raise the pitch. Since the tuner aims at producing distinct pitches, as he carves and sharpens the slabs, he tests for pitch level. As soon as he hears the pitches he is seeking, he stops tampering with the slabs. That is why slabs are rarely finished as a result of this construction method. Among the Nwoge group of the Igbo, xylophone slabs are tuned to the heptatonic scale. On this instrument, the third and the seventh notes are used as neutral notes. Neutral notes are sounding notes of indefinite pitches, and they are used in Igbo music for producing non-musical sounds and for playing *ostinato.* As the xylophone performs dual function—melodic and rhythmic, the neutral notes fulfill the rhythmic functions of the instrument.

The tuning system under *ikpo* (plucked or bowed instruments) is by tightening or loosening the strings to the desired pitch. The tuning of instruments under *ifu* (wind instruments) consists of carving and shaping to a particular culturally accepted form. The instruments are made from a variety of materials ranging from animal horns, elephant tusks, human bones, calabash, wood, bamboo canes, and grass stalks. The material of which the instrument is made also determines the instrument's musical and cultural functions.

One year after the release of the above article, Joy published a similar essay that complements the aforementioned, titled, "Classification of

Igbo Musical Instruments."[30] The purpose of this essay is to find ways of incorporating Nigerian instruments in a national musical effort; hence, the methodology is derived from indigenous terminologies and concepts. Some few Western familiar terms such as Sachs-Hornbostel system are interjected to elucidate certain aspects of the discussion and to place Nigerian instruments in a global purview. Among the Igbo in Nigeria, the classification of musical instruments takes two factors into consideration. The first factor deals with the classification of the instruments based upon how they are played, and the second with the various functions of the instruments in the indigenous context. The Igbo grouped their instruments into five major forms—*iyo* (to shake, rattle, or clap together), *iku* (to strike a hard surface with a beater), *iti* (to strike a membrane with hand or beater), *ikpo* (to pluck or bow), and *ifu* (to blow). The roles or functions of these instruments in Igbo society is generally divided into three main categories: (1) rhythmic, (2) melodic, and (3) rhythmo-melodic.[31] The second part of the essay describes in detail various Igbo musical instruments under the five indigenous nomenclatures.

Joy continued her quest to demystify the perception of indigenous musical instruments in Nigeria, in particular, of the Igbo ethnic group. Hence, in 1984, she published another article on this topic, "Performance Practice in Nigerian Music."[32] The study discusses performance practice in Nigerian traditional music, focusing on three Igbo instruments—the *oja* (flute), the *ubo-aka* (thumb piano), and the *ngedegwu* (xylophone). The essay is based on the premise that in traditional African society, music is functional and that it constitutes an integral part of life and accompanies man from birth to death. Joy delves into an elaborate

---

30 Joy Nwosu Lo-Bamijoko, "Classification of Igbo Musical Instruments," *Nigeria Magazine,* No. 144 (1983): 38-58.

31 The term "rhythmo-melodic" has been coined for use in the study to differentiate instruments whose musical functions are purely rhythmic from those that also have melodic properties.

32 Joy Nwosu Lo-Bamijoko, "Performance Practice in Nigerian Music," *Black Perspective in Music* 2, No. 12 (Spring 1984): 3-20.

discourse of two categorical levels of music function, that is, social and cultural. Three kinds of music have social functions: (1) religious music, (2) music for maintaining social order, and (3) recreational music. The various musics used for maintaining social order have one common feature—the sound is usually "sacred sound," that represents the voice of the gods or the voice of the spirits of the ancestors. Recreational music includes all categories of dance music—wrestling music, music for moonlight games, music for serenading, masquerade music, work songs, music used by women for company, music used by men for relaxation, and music used for praising or satirizing people.

Among the Igbo of Nigeria, the cultural and social functions of music intertwine and complement one another. Music functions culturally in the areas of ritual, ceremony, and social life. Rituals in Igbo culture involve inner-chamber spiritual or ancestral rites not open to the public. Ceremonial music encompasses both the inner- and outer-chamber levels. Following this explanations, Joy went on to discuss each of the three musical instruments, highlighting their organology, philosophy of sonic production, performance etiquettes, and their functions in the Igbo culture.

1984 turns out to be a very busy and productive year for Joy. She published another article in this year; this time on "Music Education in Nigeria."[33] In this essay, Joy discusses music education in Nigeria under nine sub-topics: (1) education in the traditional society, (2) music in traditional education, (3) music in informal education, (4) non-musical rhythms of life, (5) musical rhythms of life, (6a) music in formal education—initiation into manhood, (6b) initiation into womanhood, (7) contemporary music education in Nigeria, (8) music education and Nigerian schools, and (9) music education at the university level. In traditional African society, education catered to the whole humankind, his/her mental, spiritual, and physical life, and each stage of education has music as its stabilizing force. In a traditional non-literate culture,

---

33   Joy Nwosu Lo-Bamijoko, "Music Education in Nigeria," *Nigeria Magazine* 150 (1984): 40-47.

music served the same purpose as writing in the literate world. As a result of this, it was the aim of every member of a traditional society to know and understand the languages of music. There are two kinds of musical languages—non-musical rhythms of life and musical rhythms of life. At the level of non-musical rhythms of life, the language of music starts from the time a child is conceived. The heartbeat has its own rhythm, and this rhythm puts into motion and controls the whole rhythm of the body; that is, the whole of life's activities is body rhythm, such as walking, pounding, talking, and the child learns to react to all these inherent rhythms of life.

By the time the African reaches the stage of the musical rhythms of life, he/she has learned to comprehend, respond, and reproduce in concrete ways such as tapping the top of the table or beating the drum—those rhythmic patterns that have been an integral part of his/her life. As the child grows up, she/he is watching, listening and learning; and when he/she is alone, he/she is reliving the experience on any object that is at hand. Children in communities can be heard trying out drum rhythms on walls, on trees, even on their thighs, or on one another's heads. Meanwhile, in the community, life goes on, and drums are seen performing social functions other than informing and teaching. Initiation into manhood in traditional African society prepares the boys to become men. Most professional training begins long before the training for the attainment of manhood. This includes training as a musician. By the time a man reaches manhood, he already knows what his profession in life would be, and the period of training that prepares him for life also prepares him for his calling.

During initiation into womanhood, groups of young girls in training were taught women's music among other things. At the end of the initiation period, the girls normally staged a coming of age dance. All men of marrying age, that is, prospective suitors, attended this dance to choose their future wives. At the end of this section of the essay, Joy sadly points out that most of what are reported above had changed, both for men and women. The extent of these changes and the result of the changes could be seen in the big cosmopolitan cities where most of what have been discussed is non-existent.

As regards contemporary music education in Nigeria, the essay highlights some of the most popular modern dance music such as highlife, *juju, akwete, waka, apala,* and *sakara.* Today, music education is becoming very fashionable in Nigeria. By music education, it means the Western music as it is known and practiced in the European countries and America. Upper-middle-class and affluent parents desire their children to learn music. This usually consists of piano, organ, violin, or voice. Apart from the university music programs, the only other way of receiving music tutelage in Nigeria is through the services of private music instructors or church. This is because music is not one of the regular subjects in the Nigerian school curricular. To minimize the problems created by the lack of music teachers in Nigeria, the Nigerian government, in 1961, established a music department at the University of Nigeria, Nsukka. The university program is still not able to create ideal music curricular in the elementary and high schools as envisaged. At the base of this lack of progress is the underlying confusion about what type of music Nigeria should teach its pupils, whether traditional or Western music.

The next article published in 1985, "Conversation on African Music: Leslie R. Saunders Interviews Joy Nwosu Lo-Bamijoko,"[34] has a very interesting background. When Joy returned from Michigan in 1982, the Head of the Department of Music at the University of Nigeria, Nsukka, invited her to join their teaching staff as a 'music instructor.' Joy was baffled because, she already had her Ph.D. in music, and was being invited to become a 'music instructor!' It was clear to Joy that she was not considered good enough to become a lecturer. Joy, very politely declined. By that time, she was already a Lecturer in Music at the University of Lagos. The then Head of the Department of Music at

---

34   Leslie R. Saunders, "Conversation on African Music: Leslie R. Saunders Interviews Joy Nwosu Lo-Bamijoko," *Music Educators Journal* 71, No. 9 (1985): 57-59.

the University of Nigeria, an English man, left Nsukka some years later and returned to England.

Joy subscribes to the *Music Educators Journal* from the time she was a student at Michigan. She was surprised to read an article by this former head of the music at Nsukka that was so denigrating of Nigerian music. He purportedly went to Nigeria to develop in Nigerians the sense of good music; by good music, he meant Western classical music. In his report, he alleged that his Nigerian students had no ear for musical tone, that is Western music, and that they sang out of pitch. There was so much vilification of the Nigerian music in that article that Joy was infuriated and wanted to respond and call him names. Joy wanted to accuse him of having wasted his years in Nigeria trying to force the people to learn his musical culture, but missed the opportunity to learn the musical culture of the people of Nigeria. Joy felt sorry for him for such a lost privilege. She knew that if she had attacked him, she would have lost the battle, and will probably not have her rebuttal accepted or published. Instead of attacking him directly, Joy chose to instruct him about Nigerian music by castigating the corrigenda, so that he could see what he missed. That refutation was the result of the article below. In fact, he had planned to publish a series of articles on his sojourn in Nigeria, but Joy's article truncated his fallacious reports on Nigerian music.

In this interview-article, Leslie Saunders asked Joy thirteen cogent questions to enunciate the understanding of African music, in particular, music of Nigeria. Joy upholds the function of melody and rhythm as the two factors that distinguish African music from Western music. Melody in African music is based on the choice and arrangement of tones derived from the sound of the spoken word—logogenic. Rhythm is to the traditional African musician as melody is to the Western musician. Joy believes that African music is well organized with rules as the Western classical music. For illustration, when composing vocal song, the text always precedes the music. Where the composer chooses to write the music before the text, she/he must eventually adjust the sound to mirror the contour of the words. In addition, African traditional music tends to be monadic in nature—a syllable per sound.

In the area of counterpoint, Joy affirms that the most prevalent style in African vocal music is still "call-and-response" technique. As regards instrumental music, each instrument of the orchestra plays a specific musical role, and their patterns or parts form *ostinato* to those that play the solo roles. In African traditional instrumental music, counterpoint takes place in the "hocket" technique used by some flute ensembles. In Western music, harmony and melody are often more important that the underlying rhythm. Likewise, in African music, rhythm and melody are equally important, because melody is the actual music, while rhythm enhances melody. Joy explains that African music is conceived horizontally, that is, melodically in linear form, and not vertically as music of harmonic nature in Western music. Harmony in African music can result from two or more horizontal movements of parallel thirds. This form of harmony is important in choral music.

2011 was a special year for Joy. She published her fourth book, *Mirror of Our Lives: Voices of Four Igbo Women.*[35] In this book, four Nigerian women share the compelling tales of their troubled lives and failed marriages, revealing how each managed to not only survive, but triumph under difficult and repressive circumstances. Njide, Nneka, Miss Nelly, and Oby relive their stories of passion, deceit, heartaches, and strength, as they push through life—each on a unique odyssey to attain happiness, self-respect, and inner peace. But none of the women's journeys is without misjudgments and missteps. Njide falls in love at first sight, marries Tunji too quickly, and is dismayed when Tunji shows his true colors. Nneka once thought that she and Oji were the perfect couple, until Oji traveled to the United States. Miss Nelly is a kind and good natured woman who allows everyone to take advantage of her, even her husband, whom she married only for his name. But everyone wonders why Oby and Mat married at all, for their marriage was a battle

---

35 Joy Nwosu Lo-Bamijoko, *Mirror of Our Lives: Voices of Four Igbo Women* (Bloomington, IN: iUniverse Publishing, 2011).

from the very beginning. The tales in *Mirror of Our Lives: Voices of Four Igbo Women* will inspire women around the world to never give up, to discover a sense of worth, and most of all, to learn to love themselves above everything else.

In addition to her astute contributions in reputable music journals, Joy published several short essays on popular music, music industry, social life, traditional culture, and politics, in Nigerian magazines and Newspapers such as *Megastar, African Notes, Music in Nigeria, The Guardian, Sunday Punch, Lagos Life, Sunday Times,* and *National Concord.* Some of the topics of her essays include, "Music and Recreation," "A Meditation Upon a Festival," "Nigerian Traditional Hairstyles," "The Mmanwu Drama," "I Come from Utopia," "CMA at Induction Course for Music Teachers," "Simply NEPA[36]," "Joy Nwosu," "Black Emancipation," and "Why Junk Music Thrives."

---

36   NEPA = Nigeria Electric Power Authority.

Chapter 4

Concert Performances

As an operatic soprano, Joy Nwosu thrilled the selective classical music *aficionados* in Nigeria, Ghana, United Kingdom, Italy, and the United States, with her God-gifted voice that is best described as *bel canto*. She performed several *arias* from well-known operas by Handel, Mozart, Gluck, Bononcini, Puccini, Verdi, Faure, Bankole, Ekwueme, Fiberesima, and *lieder* of Schubert, Schumann, Duke, and Grieg.

Joy is one of the first professionally trained sopranos in Nigeria to successfully conjoin the rendition of European classical repertoire with indigenous folk songs, and popular dance music. As a result, Joy had performed to small classical audiences, large crowd of popular music, and at times, she combined the three styles of music in a single concert, and interestingly, her audiences never got bored. They always shout for an *en core* at the end of such a rarity. Her performances were eclectic, electrifying, flawless, and patriotic. Nigerian journalists have crowned Joy "first lady of sound," "diva," *"maestro,"* and "high priestess of Nigerian music;" titles that she rightfully earned and deserved for three reasons: (1) Joy was the first professionally trained female musician in Nigeria to combine operatic singing with popular dance music; (2) she was the first trained female musician to set up a dance band in Nigeria;

and (3), Joy was the first trained female musician to release a Long Playing record in Nigeria. Below are selected reviews of some of Joy's stellar performances from Nigerian local and national newspapers.

The Center for Cultural Studies, University of Lagos, will be putting up a Night of Folk Music on Friday, 22 October, 1976. The Center was conceived principally as a place for the performing arts. Activities of the center will take place around the Haile Sellasie Auditorium and the Arts Theater of the University of Lagos. Regular activities of professional standard in drama, dance, music, and fine arts, will be staged in these venues. Interactions between the university and performing groups in the city of Lagos as well as other parts of the country will also be encountered. Although, the center will employ its own artists and musicians, it is also hoped that interested artists, musicians, and dancers employed in other fields would be invited on part-time basis to participate in productions and workshops.

The night of the 22nd will not only feature that versatile international singer, Joy Nwosu, but also the great Bayo Martins, another firm believer in the functionalities of music. For an African music in the classical sense of the word—its norms and standards, as intended by the Western world, means nothing, unless, when it begins to inspire in him, those familiar sentiments and moods that he recognizes. This is so when we talk of spontaneity. But to fully involve the African in music, he has to be able to identify his own feelings and moods, with those that music tries to express, especially, where music begins to take on other functions apart from dance.

It has been argued many times, even by the Africans themselves, that music has one major function in our culture, and that is dance. That is why we dance to celebrate births as well as deaths. It has also been argued that any function short of this is alien to our culture. This is one argument that some musicians in this country have been trying to debunk, and this program is a contribution to that effect. This is basically the idea behind Joy's music, an idea Bayo Martins, the exponent of the generative rhythms of Africa, shares. Also involved in the Cultural Center Instrumental Ensemble are some great musicians such as Dele Bamgbose, Rocky, and Igo Chico.[37]

One of Nigeria's musicians and singers is Joy Nwosu. Apart from the television and several records that are fast gaining popularity, she is a performer rarely seen live; that is a great pity. At the designated weekend, I chose to be at the Italian Embassy to listen and watch her perform. She was backed by her band and the Performing Arts Troupe of the University of Lagos. Although, the program was almost an hour behind schedule; that was soon forgotten by the appearance of her band that started off by playing the popular Tanzanian song, "Malaeka." I thought it was going to be more than "a night of Nigerian folk songs," and feared an impending boredom as I glanced through the program that indicated only Igbo folk songs. Looking at the rather international gathering of members of the diplomatic corps, I feared even more; but I was wrong. We sat stiff at the beginning, but gradually began to relax as we became part of that intimate world created by this "high priestess" of music. How did she do it? The feat was achieved through a combination of music, ritual, dance, diverse moods, story telling, and the expression of all those feelings with her voice. Practically, all her songs were accompanied by interpretative dances with the band fully identifying the mood of the singers until the audience got carried away completely.

The first number she performed was a ritual to the goddess of moonlight to create the world in which fantasy reigns supreme. The two dancers were Isaac Ojium and Toyin Ajetunmobi. Joy herself joined in narrating the story. When finally she got into the song, the audience understood. The feelings in the songs were also well-expressed by the accompanying dances, in this way, the audience never felt left out. From the story of the deserted lover—Okwudili, to the song of prisoners, to the song in honor of the thumb pianist—Egwu Ubo, and to the story of the most beautiful dancer; we were convinced it was all part of the

---

37　"Night of Folk Music and Excitement," *Evening Times,* Tuesday, 19 October, 1976.

same world in which we live. There was a short break in which the band took over playing popular highlife tunes from even far away Ghana.

The second part opened to a beautiful number, "Egwu-Umu-Agbogho," that was the maiden dance and appropriately three girls did an alluring dance. This was taking over by "The Call," expressing the silent anger of a loving woman in discord with her spouse. The most heart-warming number was "Ife di N'ioba," a caricature of women folk. The interpretative dance was staged by a male member of the troupe, dressed and made-up to mimic the excesses of some modern women. The woman was seen as loud, quarrelsome fellow, who drinks and smokes too much, keeps late hours and bad company. The last number "Ile," was a warning about some of the social vices such as rumor mongering, and too soon, the program smoothly came to an end. The rapport and rapt attention she exerted was due mainly to her ability to keep the audience engrossed. Even while changing her costumes, music and dance continued.

There was never a break in the story and the atmosphere remained piquant, long after the performance was over. Joy Nwosu who has won several prizes both at home and abroad, had a classical training in Italy, where she obtained the highest licentiate in music and voice. Her vocal quality and delivery earned her the title, *maestro*. One question that came to my mind was why should such a talent be restricted to the Ivory Tower? Joy, as a performer, should be exposed more not only on the theater stage, but to the cabaret and the night clubs, where she could best utilize the intimate atmosphere she creates that fully involves the feelings of her audience, as demonstrated at the Italian Embassy.[38]

Nearly five years ago, Joy Nwosu stepped down from the stage after performing the "greatest show ever organized by an individual artist in this country." Still, artists and their promoters are trying to meet the standard she set and recapture those thrilling moments of "Show Unlimited." Since then, lovers of the musical and theatrical arts have been punctuating the recently increased list of stage and

---

38 "Joy is a Thriller Any Day," *Daily Times,* Thursday, 22 December, 1977.

television performers with queries of "where is Joy?" Some have blamed her increased family responsibilities, for she has since started a family. Some have blamed her academic obligations, for she has since earned her doctorate degree, and aside from university lecturing, she is a prolific writer, a researcher, and has no less than ten full-time voice students. The criticism, if there is to be any actually lies with the present business climate, and attitude of "businessmen" in the country. Sponsors are hard to come by, and a performer of Joy's caliber needs sponsorship. The cost of quality productions has spiked since 1978, and Joy refuses to lower her standard. Consequently, she may perform and the public does not hear about it until too late.

Such would probably be the case of her free special Christmas Concert coming up, had the Nigerian Television Authority—NTA, not stepped in. This concert will entertain, inspire, and complement the Christmas spirit with songs. The hour-long program will feature a mixture of African and European Christmas music. Among the works of Nigerian composers to be featured are compositions by the late Ayo Bankole and Prof. Akin Euba. There will also be sing along of popular Christmas carols. A similar concert will be held today at Saint Dominic's Catholic Church, Yaba, Lagos, at 7:30 PM. Although, this too is a free concert, donations will be taken for the building fund of the joint Catholic/Protestant Chapel being built on the campus of the University of Lagos at Akoka. Both performances will feature piano accompanist, Richard Bucknor, and a chorus and ensemble of music students from the Department of Music, University of Lagos.[39]

Definitely not all, but there will certainly be a lot of Nigeria presented in a musical form when Joy Nwosu mounts the podium on Tuesday, 1 October, 1985. In an Independence Day expose, organized by the Black Artists Corporation—BAC, the singer better known for the ripples she has caused in the realm of folk music will sing in a myriad of media, spanning European classical, folk, and popular music. The show that will come up at the auditorium of the University of Lagos, will be a

39   "Joy's Christmas Treat," *Daily Times*, 17 December, 1983.

concert of epic proportion, in the sense that Joy will take all of eight hours to give the audience what she feels it deserves. But as she explains it, those who will take time to come will not have to tight on their seats throughout the duration. Rather, a three-part program is planned; each spans two hours, with an allowance for an hour break after the first and second parts.

The show is billed to start at noon, and Joy, now a Senior Lecturer in Music at UNILAG, will sing classical songs written by such house-hold names as the late Ayo Bankole, Adam Fiberesima, Lazarus Ekwueme, and others. The second part will feature the band performing works by Adeolu Akinsanya, Bobby Benson, Victor Olaiya, Roy Chicago, Zeal Onyia, Eddy Okonta, Israel Nwoba, Hubert Udemba, Chris Ibeto, Ebenezer Obey, Sunny Ade, Fela Anikulapo-Kuti, and a host of other past and present popular musicians. She will be accompanied by a band of twenty-five musicians and a choral set.[40]

---

40 "Joy Nwosu Sings for Nigeria," *The Guardian Supplement*, Sunday, 22 September, 1985.

Joy Nwosu in Concert at the Main Auditorium of the University of Lagos, 1985.

Nigeria's first-lady of sound, Joy Nwosu Lo-Bamijoko, will present a show of some of the finest veteran performances in Nigeria on 1 October, 1985, in a concert that will last eight hours to celebrate Nigeria's twenty-fifth anniversary. Joy is taking the lead. The day will start off with popular art songs written by Nigerian and Western composers such as Ayo Bankole sr., Adam Fiberesima, and Lazarus Ekwueme. Since some songs will come from the opera, she will present them in special costumes and settings. It is a show that is promising to thrill the hearts of the audience. Adeolu Akinsanya, Bobby Benson, Victor Olaiya, Roy Chicago, Zeal Onyia, Eddy Okonta, Stephen Amaechi, Celestine Ukwu, Victor Uwaifo, Sunny Okosun, Osita Osadebe, Inyang Henshaw, Rex Lawson, Israel Nwoba, Hubert Ubemba, Christopher Ibeto, I. K. Dairo, Ebenezer Obey, Sunny Ade, and Fela Anikulapo-Kuti, are composers that you will be hearing their music performed by Joy's instrumental band during the second part of this mammoth event. The orchestra will be performing selected popular songs from 1960 to 1985. It will be an historical survey of popular music since independence. The evening will be rounded up with folk songs composed by Joy. Some of her most beautiful and thought provoking songs will be on display. She will mount the stage with twenty-five musicians, a dance troupe, and special guest performers.[41]

Joy Nwosu belongs in that unique company of Nigerian popular musicians who received their formal training in European music. Schooled in the classical tradition of Italian grand opera, she was a soprano of distinction when she returned to Nigeria in 1972 to begin her career. The pattern of her career is the usual one—early talent recognition; a scholarship to the best school of the conservatories in Europe; academic distinction; return home, and a false start in the European tradition; crisis of non-acceptance by the home audience; a fresh apprenticeship, this time, in African traditional music; persistence through a difficult transition; and finally, rebirth into a new musical

---

41 "Eight-Hour Concert Billed for Independence Anniversary," *New Nigeria*, Saturday, 28 September, 1985.

universe. To date, she has produced four LP records and a fifth is in process.

Joy Nwosu, who in private life is Mrs. Lo-Bamijoko, makes four basic complaints about the music industry in Nigeria today:

1. Recording companies are not interested in what an artist can get. They tap his resources for quick turn-over without nurturing him. Raw talents are not trained as is the case abroad.

2. The contract policy of recording companies is absurd and different from what obtains elsewhere in the world. Potential artists are signed on for three years, but no retainer fee is paid to them. Such contracts prevent them from recording elsewhere. Our artists do not know their rights in this connection and it strangles them. As soon as they are finished, the companies make hasty replacements to continue their exploitation.

3. Reliable sources have proved that these recording companies have established a very strong union that they use to make and unmake artists. It is unfortunate that this kind of thing is allowed to happen in Nigeria. If our artists realize the extent of their power, they would be making the rules, not the companies. It is irresponsible for these companies to unionize for the sole purpose of exploiting musicians. They have no right to punish artists whether such artists are hated or not. It is for the audience to decide which artist gets popular or not.

4. The government attitude to the arts in general is discouraging. A lot of people, who are not qualified, use the professional title of "musician" which may explain why government hardly takes them seriously. Government fails to realize that talent alone does not make the artist. That is why very little emphasis is laid on training. There are uncountable people with talents who lack the basic entry qualifications into institutions of higher learning.

But Joy Nwosu did not find fault only with the government and recording companies. She also gave her fellow artists some tick-off. According to her, the financial success of certain musicians went to their heads and for that they equate wealth with artistic perfection. Joy further said that all classes of Nigerian musicians are guilty of conceit. "The musician with no academic training thinks that the success of his LP has turned him into an instant expert in music. The academic musicians themselves believe that their chain of degrees give them sweeping knowledge into the realms of music, particularly the traditional forms. It happened to me too." However, Mrs. Lo-Bamijoko learned her mistakes soon after she returned from her training in Rome. Few people appreciated her concerts then. Lots of others wondered why she would not sing what they could share with her. At first, she resisted their appeal, but ultimately she succumbs and came down from the Ivory Tower. "At that time," she said, "I was a producer at NBC. I became an apprentice with the *Atomic 8 Band* that was led by Dan Satch. For one and half years, I had this band at my disposal, singing. When the band left for the Eastern states, I joined Segun Ayoola's *The Satisfactions* for another year. That was how I learned the African way of singing. I learned what it was to sing with a different vocal texture to make it African."

Joy Nwosu's musical career so far falls into two phases. From 1973 to 1978, she released four LPs. The most outstanding of these was her first record, *Uwam,* a pathos—laden rendition of her emotions at the death of her loved ones during the civil war. The second and present stage started after her doctorate studies in the United States in 1981. Her training in the United States has contributed a lot to her new singing, especially in the art of being able to sing with such clarity and elocution that every word is distinctly heard. Joy Nwosu's post United States album is nearing completion. Judging from the demonstration cassette, there is a distinct freshness and clarity in her singing. This success she owes to a group of jazz singers whom she described as one of the best in America: "Their style of singing is close to our own. I appreciated all the more that different voices were necessary for singing in Igbo and local idioms. I saw that the voice can sing anything that instruments could play."[42] Another interesting point about the upcoming album is Mrs. Lo-Bamijoko's almost total reliance on traditional instruments. Joy's singing was accompanied by a xylophone. There were also the melodic instruments such as conga, talking drum, another drum and the *ogene*—iron bell. The western instruments used were a guitar, saxophone, and a trumpet.[43]

This weekend, the National Theater, Iganmu, Lagos, will witness one of those rare occasions when one of Nigeria's celebrated song writer and star performer comes back with a bang. She is Joy Nwosu, the singer who had her last full stage production seven years ago. But this time around, she will be featuring among a cast of thirty-five performers with special guests such as BJ (I go die o), J. R. Mitchell, Ahmed Omar, to entertain the audience. The show will be hosted for two days, Saturday and Sunday, with three shows each day beginning from 12 noon. The first show will comprise dramatic musical scenes complete with costumes, and settings of selected scenes from classical operas, including *Aida, Marriage of Figaro, La Traviata, Turandot, Opu Jaja* by Adam Fiberesima, *Night of Miracles* by Ayo Bankole, and a *Night in Bethlehem* by Lazarus Ekwueme.

The second show of the day will be dedicated to the popular music of Nigeria from 1960 to 1985, with the band playing music of over twenty-six popular music composers. The third part will feature Joy Nwosu's own poignant compositions. She has packaged a unique combination of gospel, folk, and revolutionary songs that are sure to stir the audience. These selections according to her are tightly molded into an interesting story of a people's willingness to struggle for independence while praying

---

42 Scat singing is a vocal technique in which the human voice imitates musical instruments in jazz music. This phrase was coined by the legend and father of jazz, Louis Armstrong.

43 Chucks Iloegbunam, "Music Conversation with Joy Nwosu," *The Guardian*, Wednesday, 20 November, 1985.

to God and man for peace. As Lagos awaits the D-day, the big question is, why would someone go through the trouble to put up a show like this in Nigeria, where the arts are unfortunately not well supported? Joy Nwosu simply says: "I am trained in this particular field—stage production. To me, it is a job, and being a job under any circumstances."[44]

Joy Nwosu is one entertainer who can give you more than enough treat anytime she is on stage. Watching her perform at the main hall of the National Theater, on 26 October, 1985, one witnessed stage craftsmanship, without doubt, inspired by expertise and hard work. Joy spent about three months putting the two-day concert together—her contribution to the celebration of our silver jubilee independence. Call it a marathon performance—she aptly christened it so, and you are not wrong as it was a six-hour affair incorporating music, dance, and drama from mid-day through six in the evening. The business of the day wrapped into segments of three. The first part was of classical music in which there were selections from popular songs by Nigerian and Western composers and taking a dip into the operas too. The scenes from the classics were dramatized; for instance, "So Ri Na Te Me Bo," an excerpt from Adam Fiberesima's *Opu Jaja*. Here, King Jaja, Prince Jaja, and a representative of the British Council converged to discuss. Just then, the king's wife walks in to announce a looming danger on the inland and of invasion.

Turning to Giuseppe Verdi—from Italy, Joy takes *Pace, Pace, Mio Dio* in *La Forza Del Destino*. Here, Leonora tries to elope with her lover Dan Alvaro. This plan is uncovered by her father Marquis of Calatrava. Alvaro regrets their hatched plan, throws aside his pistol that in the process goes off, killing Marquis. Leonora disguises as a man, seeking refuge in a monastery where she prays that this incident is forgotten. In all these scenes from the European classics, Joy ensures that comprehension is aided through miming. Understanding is further reinforced by the narration that precedes the commencement of each scene. Altogether, eleven scenes were featured. Worthy of note is the elaborate use of costumes depicting the various times the scenes recreated took place.

---

44 "Joy Nwosu Performs," *National Concord*, Saturday, 26 October, 1985.

To heighten the spectacle, Joy seems to have taken care of the apathy that should have arisen because of the incomprehension of European classical operas by some members of the audience. Indeed, Joy Nwosu distinguished herself as an operatic soprano. Speaking with her later while on break, I queried myself if she was the same lady who sang in those high pitches a while ago. We talked: "The voice is an instrument," she told me. That she could manipulate? Yes, "I want people to love opera. That is why Bola Johnson comes out to interpret. All opera is music drama. I wish I could sing it in our languages." Calling for interest in opera, Joy says criticisms are tolerated: "We can meet half-way in order to improve." I should think in this first segment she enjoyed the parts played by Emmanuel Tettey—baritone, Richard Bucknor—piano, and Ernest Boamah—piano.

More treats as Joy's band took the audience down memory lane with popular highlife tunes, flavored highlife music that dominated the air waves in yesteryears, but still, nevertheless, retaining its popular appeal. Joy did not sing in this segment of the concert. Rather, she stayed behind the scene as her back-up band played, dishing out those favorites you used to hear in the 1960s. Recall them—Bobby Benson's "Taxi Driver," ("If You Marry Taxi Driver, I Don't Care"), Inyang Henshaw's "Ekorokpete," Rex Lawson's "Love Adure," etc. The nostalgia generated by this highlife session was rather inundating. It is pertinent, therefore, to extend due credit to the back-up musicians and the lady dancers cum singers. Of course, Juju and afro-beat music earned recognition too. Popular numbers by I. K. Dairo, Ebenezer Obey, Sunny Ade, and Fela Anikulapo-Kuti's "Palaver," came up in this category. Towards the end of the show, it was time for Joy Nwosu to render her compositions. Here, the singer turns to folklores. The songs were captivating to the extent that they drew loud applause from the audience. At the end of the day, one felt entertained, appraising the show in its entirety. Joy sings to your satisfaction. She could hold your attention for as long as she wishes, given her skillfulness.[45]

---

45   Joseph Dominic, "Joy Nwosu at the National Theater," *The Guardian*, Wednesday, 20 November, 1985.

Joy Nwosu at City Hall, Lagos, 1974.

Joy Nwosu at Randall Hall, Lagos, 1976.

Joy Nwosu at Randall Hall, Lagos, 1976.

Joy Nwosu at Randall Hall, Lagos, 1976.

Joy Nwosu at Enugu Government House, 1985.

Joy Nwosu at Randall Hall, Lagos, 1987.

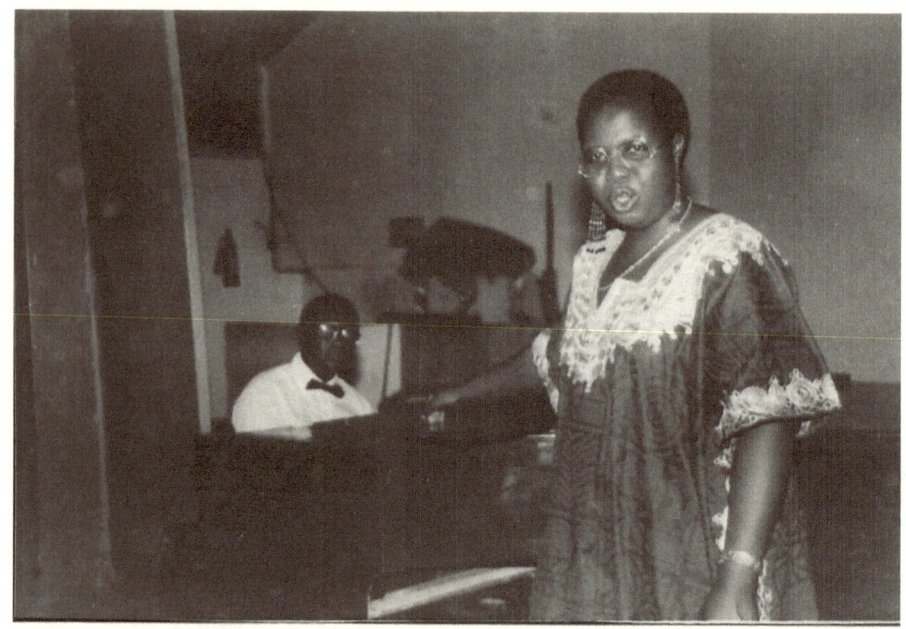

Joy Nwosu and Richard Bucknor at Randal Hall, Lagos, 1987.

Joy Nwosu Meets Ben Enwonwu[46] at Randall Hall, Lagos, 1987.

---

46   Benedict Chuka Enwonwu (1921 - 1994), better known as Ben Enwonwu, was
an Igbo, Nigerian painter and sculptor.

117

Chapter 5

Encomiums

Joy Nwosu has been eulogized and decorated with several accolades from competitions, distinguished organizations, eminent personalities, institutions, and the diplomatic corps, in Africa, Europe, and the United States. These encomiums attest to her impeccable accomplishments and contributions to African ethnomusicology, educational policies, cultural matters, political views, and more importantly, for her trailblazing efforts to liberate Nigerian women from subjugation to their male counterparts. Joy flourished in the very arenas that were exclusively dominated by men and she prevailed in most of the obstacles thrown at her to decimate her aspirations. Below is a selected eulogies bestowed on Joy Nwosu.

Letters of Praise

M.O. Eperokun, former Registrar of the University of Lagos, in the confirmation of appointment letter, dated 21 August, 1978, writes: "I have the pleasure in informing you that the Appointments and Promotions Board at its meeting held on 25 July, 1978, approved the recommendation that your appointment be confirmed.[47] On behalf of

---

47   Confirmed = Tenured.

the Vice-Chancellor, I congratulate you on this confirmation of your appointment and hope that you will continue to put your best into the service of the university."

I. O. Ajijola, former Acting Registrar of the University of Lagos, in the promotion letter dated 26 July, 1985, writes: "I have the pleasure in informing you that the Appointments and Promotions Board at its meeting held on 4 July, 1985, approved the recommendation that you be promoted to Senior Lecturer with effect from 1 October, 1985… On behalf of the Vice-Chancellor, I congratulate you very heartily on this promotion and hope that you will feel stimulated and encouraged by this recognition of your work in the university and that this will spur you on to greater output."

In a letter for the SOLIDRA[48] Award 1991, from the Chairman and Honorable Secretary, The SOLIDRA Circle, Lagos, drops this line: "The SOLIDRA Circle, Lagos, has selected you as a recipient for its Individual Award for your contribution to Art – in Dramatic and Performing Arts for the 1991 SOLIDRA Award. It is hoped that you would be able to accept the award and be present at the Award Ceremony that will take place at the Federal Palace Hotel, Victoria Island, Lagos, on Friday, 6 December, 1991, between the hours of 6:00 PM and 11:00 PM …"

Anne McLellan, former administrator and secretary of the Commonwealth Music Association, London, writes about Joy: "In 1991, Joy Nwosu Lo-Bamijoko was instrumental in setting up the Nigerian Chapter of the Commonwealth Music Association and became our national representative in Nigeria. Joy worked extremely hard in setting up links with the Nigeria government and eventually the chapter was accepted by the Ministry of Education as one of their subventions. They are now jointly planning to publish the Nigerian Music Directory, compiled and edited by Joy Nwosu. As our representative in Nigeria, Joy was accepted by the Commonwealth Foundation for their Commonwealth Fellowship in 1993. She also gave invaluable support

---

48   SOLIDRA = Social Literary Dramatic Circle, Lagos, Nigeria.

and advice to our then General Secretary, who, with the Royal Overseas League and the Commonwealth Foundation, organized and presented a Gala Concert for Her Majesty the Queen, to celebrate her anniversary as Head of the Commonwealth. As one of our active representatives, Joy has now been elected as our new General Secretary and hopefully will be able to carry on as a major inspiration to the many other representatives we have throughout the Commonwealth. Joy also continues to work very closely with the sister organization of the Commonwealth Music Association, the Center for Intercultural Music Arts, whose patrons include Chief E. C. Anyaoku and Sir Richard Luce."

Richard Donald Smith, of the United Nations International School, New York, in a referral letter, writes: "When I first met her, Dr. Lo-Bamijoko already had established herself as an authority on Igbo music and musical instruments... I was anxious to learn more about their culture through Dr. Lo-Bamijoko, herself an Igbo. I discovered that she had written many published articles on music styles, instrument classification, instrumental tunings, and other subjects which, at that time, were beneficial to my own learning. During subsequent visits to Nigeria, I observed as she took on an increasing number of important roles in the music life of Nigeria... She has also been one of the major forces behind the Nigeria chapter of the Commonwealth Music Association and the Musicological Society of Nigeria. These are scholarly organizations that attract most of the best musical minds in Nigeria. Their activities include the convening of conferences and the publishing of scholarly musicological materials. Not too long ago, one of my own articles was published in the Commonwealth Music Association Journal... Dr. Lo-Bamijoko has been extremely prolific in terms of writing and editing scholarly articles. To my own knowledge, her work spanned three continents—Africa, Europe, and North America; but it is quite possible that knowledge of her work extends even further, because the Commonwealth Music Association includes representation from all the areas of the world that formed the British Commonwealth. That could include the Far East."

In a letter for the award of the Dodge Fellowship in 1999, Ida B. Graham, Director of Licensing and Credentials, Department of Education, State of New Jersey, writes: "It is with great pleasure that I inform you that you have been selected as one of 25 recipients of a 1998-1999 Dodge Fellowship Award. The Dodge Fellowship Awards are funded by the Geraldine R. Dodge Foundation to encourage and recognize outstanding new teachers as they enter the teaching profession through New Jersey's alternative licensure program. As a Dodge Fellow, you will receive $2,000 to defray the costs of mentoring services and formal instruction that are associated with the first year of employment as an alternative licensure teacher. The Dodge Foundation Fellowships will be presented by Commissioner of Education David C. Hespe to you and your fellow recipients at the meeting of the State Board of Education on 7 April, 1999. Your school's chief administrator is being invited to accompany you to this awards presentation, that will be held at the State Department of Education's building at 100 River View Plaza in Trenton, New Jersey..."

In a letter of gratitude, dated 9 April, 1999, Dennis Sevano, Assistant Superintendent, Paterson Public School District, New Jersey, remarks: "I was extremely proud of Paterson last Wednesday when your names and resumes were read at the State Board meeting. Having a graduate of Princeton and a Ph.D. from the University of Michigan being announced as teachers from Public School #12 seemed to overshadow all the rest in a heavily packed competitive audience in Trenton..."

In another similar letter, dated 14 April, 1999, Jacqueline Farrar-Jones, Executive Assistant/PIO of the Paterson Public School District, New Jersey, showers encomiums: "On behalf of the State District Superintendent, Dr. Edwin Duroy, I extend a sincere congratulation to you on your recent recognition as one of the 1999 Geraldine R. Dodge Foundation Fellows. How exciting you must feel to be one of the recipients of such a noteworthy acknowledgement. Our students are very blessed to have such a distinguished individual as their instructor. Your credentials, background, and accomplishments, are notable and have elevated you as an outstanding first year staff member in our district. As your career continues to develop, you will be continuously rewarded for the many extra efforts you invest to promote academic excellence for Paterson's students. Please, know that the entire Paterson School District is proud of your accomplishments and more importantly, we are proud that you are a part of our school family. Best wishes for continued success."

On 26 April, 1999, Joy received a special letter of congratulations for the Dodge Fellowship Award, from the New Jersey State Senate President, Donald T. Di Francesco. He herein eulogizes Joy: "Congratulations on being the recipient of the 1998-1999 Dodge Teaching Fellowship. As the music teacher at the Paterson Public School District, you have chosen a profession that will have a tremendous impact on New Jersey's school children and on tomorrow's workforce. Your selection as one of 25 outstanding first-year teachers chosen as Dodge Fellows from a pool of nearly 300 applicants, demonstrates your strong qualifications as an educator and your profound commitment to your students. As Senate President, I appreciate your dedication to your profession and am pleased that New Jersey's children will have a teacher and role model of your caliber. Thank you for choosing to play such a large and important role in our student's future. Congratulations again on your deserved recognition, and best wishes in all of your future endeavors."

The last letter of commendation for the Dodge Fellowship came from the Surrogate of the Court House in County of Passaic, New Jersey, William J. Bate, on 7 May, 1999. In a few words, writes: "It was a delight to read that you have been chosen a Dodge Fellow. You should feel immensely proud of this distinction. Best wishes for continued fulfillment in your teaching career."

Newspaper Reviews

Nigerian journalists have written several articles about Joy's stunning career, praising her accomplishments as a popular music superstar, distinguished operatic singer, academic, music critic, teacher, trailblazer, and an icon. Below are selected reports published in some of Nigeria's most reputable national newspapers.

Her name rings a bell. She is a folk singer of no mean repute. Her singing versatility came into prominence during the NBC Cultural Night Show at the multi-million naira National Theater. I am talking about Joy Nwosu. She is on the plump side, and she solo-performed on the stage before an epic crowd, her own songs in her own joyous style. Behind her that day stood a guy who did interpret her songs into a comic dance movement and it was all ovations from the suffocating audience at the NBC night. A lecturer in music at the Center for Cultural Studies of the University of Lagos, Joy is a musical gift of that university in particular, and Nigeria in general. But being an academic does not detract from her innate humanity as a lively person, and whenever she sings, she brings feelings into her songs, sounding philosophical and carrying a load of useful message for all those who live within her cultural and ethnic repertoire.

But how does Joy Nwosu reconcile her position as a singer in an Ivory Tower? "We are fundamentally artists, just a performer who is at the same time a university teacher. And that does not in any way detract from me as a musician." Joy Nwosu has made four records, apart from her singing versatility. Her most recent and just released album called *Azania* on a Decca label is a mixture of English, Swahili, and Igbo tunes. I had an unusual interview held at her flat[49] at UNILAG campus just about midnight last week; when honest men were suppose to be sleeping. But my job took me there and we had a long talk about her life and career and all that crap. How did she come by a name like Azania for a record label? "Actually, I had a friend from South Africa whose name is Taramina—that means encouragement. I call the record Azania because it came at a time when Tanzania was the talk of the town especially with the Federal Government's strong support for Tanzania propelled me on this line of action…

---

49   Flat = apartment suite or condominium.

As for the background story of Joy Nwosu, she is Igbo and comes from Enugu-Uku, but was born in Enugu Township: "I was only four when the old man died, but my mother is still living. She is at the moment staying with me." She told me recalling the past... "*Opu Jaja* was the first thing I did when I came back from Italy in 1972, and we made *Opu Jaja* what it later became." She added with some sense of achievement.

How does she cope with her musical career? "For artists, it is very difficult to cope, doubly so for a woman, because the problems are enormous as everybody wanting to help you through your teething problems wants some favors or the other. I worked with the NBC Radio for two and half years as a producer and did many shows at the Italian Embassy. Then I joined the University of Lagos in 1975—Music Department... We performed during the FESTAC— Second World Black and African Festival of Arts and Culture, and my group did two performances. We staged a play called *Ogbanje*—a music drama. I wrote it and spiced it with some beautiful songs." Does she have any plans for the future apart from occasional recordings? "We have big plans for the future. With the two theaters—National Theater and the University of Lagos Theater, there is going to be a flurry of dramatic and musical productions. I had fought a battle in Italy where I did not lose, and coming to Nigeria, I do not intend to lose either. As I said earlier, the future is bright, the venues are there, and if we are to live by performing, I want to popularize OGBANJE, a music drama, digest it, and I am hoping that we can produce more plays and write more books."

After watching Joy Nwosu on the NBC Cultural Night, I got a feeling that she concentrates on her songs, and does little of body movement or dancing around. That seeming immobility gives her added grace and dignity, but does it not detract slightly from her musical appeal in the realm of stagecraft? Joy Nwosu says: "I am a dramatic performer and one needs all the concentration to be able to communicate with the audience. Like you said about the guy who was dancing to my tunes that night, his movements were evoking applause from the audience and that kind of spontaneous ovation was capable of unsettling my trend of thought and concentration. It was just an experiment to use him to sing my songs." Commenting on the academic front, Joy says: "In my own case, I am not part-time. I teach music and perform full-time. I am hoping that in five years time, I shall make my breakthrough, since this university has created a troupe, things will work out well for me. The idea being that, while Amadu Bello University concentrates on Dance, University of Ibadan on Drama, we at UNILAG will concentrate on Music."[50]

Joy Nwosu really is a joy to all those who come within her physical or musical orbit, and practices what she teaches as a lecturer in music at the University of Lagos, Department of Music and Art. After her acclaimed performances during the Nigerian Broadcasting Corporation's Cultural Night and the Second World Black and African Festival of Arts and Culture—FESTAC, SADNESS & JOY interviewed her. As I sat in Joy's campus flat, I saw her performing on television, and I looked around for a Video Cassette Recorder—VCR, thinking one was on. The Nigerian Television Authority was repeating excerpts from her National Theater concert, and I was given a bonus at the start of our chat, an opportunity to watch once again this musical gem of Nigeria sing with great feeling, *gusto* and charm. After her father's demise, Joy attended primary schools in Enugu and Port Harcourt, and went on to the Holy Rosary College, Enugu. She finished in 1961, but not before she had taken part in several music and drama concerts and art festivals, winning eleven silver medals and seventeen first class certificates and a silver cup.

In 1962, Joy won the then Eastern Nigerian Government Scholarship for Music, and being a devout Catholic, went on to Rome, where she studied at some of the best music colleges for ten years. Joy worked hard to earn Italy's top diploma in music, specializing in operatic singing for the theater, and returned home in 1972. The next three years saw her as

---

50   Willy Bozimo, "Joy Nwosu: A Music Star and an Ivory Tower," *Lagos Weekend*, Friday, 18 March, 1977.

a music producer with the Nigerian Broadcasting Corporation in Lagos. In 1975, she joined the University of Lagos teaching staff, and has since performed in Lagos, Port Harcourt, Enugu, and Ibadan, as well as for visiting Hungarian and Mauritian Heads of State. The NBC Cultural Night and FESTAC were the latest feathers in her cap. Joy started the Joy Nwosu Group for Research on Folk Songs of Nigeria in 1973. The group has produced four records and a current LP, *Azania*.

How does she manage to conjoin these activities with her university job? Is she not heading for compulsory retirement? "No, there is no conflict at all," she said. "In fact, when I started my job, the university gave me instructions to organize two concerts in a term.[51] I have not let them down, and have organized even more." The University of Lagos Ensemble owes its existence to Joy. The thirteen-piece band is to be expanded to a full twenty-piece orchestra. The UNILAG Performing Troupe that consists of musicians, dramatists, and dancers, is flourishing. These groups exist for the benefit of music students and the university community as a whole, and perform for charity as well. Joy Nwosu, singer and musician extraordinaire, is not shy, but she dreads ovations and the downside of fame, that she considers distracting: "Recognition on the street pulls artists away from their fans, and they go into hibernation. I do not want a situation where I will have to break away from people," she says.

I noticed that Joy's door blinds were of *adire*[52] print, and that there were batique paintings in the flat. "I do some batique painting and waxing on materials," she said. "When I was young, I used to watch and help my mother tie and dye cloth. This art helped to sustain me while I was in Italy." Joy's mother listened and occasionally smiled with pride and satisfaction as I talked to her daughter. Will Joy choose careers for her children when they arrive in the future? "I will teach music to my children from early age, but I will not dictate to them what they must

---

51   Term = Semester.

52   *Adire* = traditional tie and dye cloth.

do. If any of them wants to take up music as a career, he/she will have a sound background." And that took me to Joy's private life.

Joy is as versatile with folk songs as she is with classical music, and practices every morning. She also does a lot of breathing exercises. This is her explanation: "The day you stop practicing is the day you lose your voice," she asserted. There was a time in Africa, particularly in Nigeria, when musicians or singers were regarded as paupers and dropouts. But with academicians like Drs. Sammy Akpabot and Joy Nwosu in the trade, music has assumed new dimensions. Joy observed that young men and women have been drawing inspiration from them, and going into music. "Music has come into its own. Music is soothing and dignifying, and operatic music is aristocratic music," she says.

As regards FESTAC, Joy, who apart from performing, was Assistant Director of Music events and in charge of costumes for the Nigerian artists, thought many things went wrong with the festival that she looked on: "not as a bureaucratic thing, but as a chance for artists to practice." She expects everybody to learn from the mistakes of FESTAC, and the authorities to involve the artists in planning well in advance. She emphasized that the artists were not happy with FESTAC arrangements, and wondered where the money went when those who really mattered— the artists, did not get any. In her opinion, nothing was done for the improvement or preservation of culture. The National Theater was the artists' only consolation, providing they would be able to use it freely. Joy would like the government to create performing troupes in music, dance, and drama, as a way of preserving and furthering our real cultural heritage. Africa and the music world are blessed with the much traveled singing sensation that is Joy Ifeoma Nwosu; the girl who speaks English, Italian, French, and Spanish, and sung for high and low. She plans to sing for as long as she lives, making records, writing books, and teaching the younger generation the art and beauty of music. Nigeria and Africa have a bundle of joy in Joy Nwosu.[53]

---

53   Femi Oyewale, "She's a Joy to Hear," *Daily Times,* 1978.

An encounter with Dr. Joy Nwosu Lo-Bamijoko, opera singer, performer, music critic, and music educator at the University of Lagos, goes beyond talk on musical notes, voice texture, color, and operatic language. It is among other things, a rare change to be educated on the problems and successes, if any, of Nigeria as seen by a rare breed upwardly mobile middle-class Nigerian. This other side of her is what makes all the difference in her life. Sitting behind the desk in her small office, crammed with music books, a piano to her left, at the Arts block of the university; her simple person tend to underscore her very distinguished career as one of Nigeria's first classical music performer and music educator. Yet, another contrast is her girlish smile, rounded cheeks, and soft appearance, compared to the generous spread of silvery-grey hair that adorns her head. Nothing to do with her age; just another unique feature in a woman of note who dared to read music in the very early 1960s when professions like law and medicine were the ultimate subjects for any brilliant student.

Joy Nwosu in Her Office at the University of Lagos, 1990.

A woman of music, she discusses politics of the land with the insight of a seasoned politician. Because she too with all her achievements is caught on the wrong side of time, she feels that strain of Structural Adjustment Program (SAP) awaits a chance… Once the discussion veered into politics and governance, that girlish smile gives way to a very angry look. One with a lot of concern for a great country, blessed abundantly, but just waiting to be properly directed. She believes, illiteracy is the main reason there has not been a fundamental change: "It is not surprising then that all the organs of education like radio and television are seriously controlled by government to serve their own selfish ends," she says…

"I am happy I came out of it alive. I could have been dead," she explains. "Intrigues are too much in the civil service. There is a status quo nobody wants to change because of the multiplier effect. Hence, everything is geared towards protecting that status quo." With concern written all over her face, she went on to narrate how her files would disappear and she would not find anybody to hold responsible. That even when they reappear most times, the contents are either altered or missing… Lo-Bamijoko explains that the situation was nightmarish: "It was a situation where you can only do as much as they want you to do," she says. "You cannot work at your own pace. I do not think we need a system that deters progress." She recommends a complete overhaul of the system, "even if it will kill us." "I know heads will roll, but things have to really get bad to improve."

Towards the end of her bickering with the system, as if listening to an inner warning system or a voice of caution, she stops. All that anger begins to fade away but not before saying, "there is so much one can say about a system. We happen to have a country where if you say too much you can lose your life. One has to watch what one says. There is a proverb in my place that says, if you fight and run away, you live longer. It is not a sign of weakness but of strength. You run away so you can fight again. I have said enough for now." Asked if this means she will never work in government again, she says: "If what I saw at Anambra State and NTA is showing in that British television series, "Yes Minister," is what government is all about; then I do not want to be a part of it. I rather be in the pressure group and work as an artist to contribute my quota."[54]

It was a frosty morning. The January harmattan[55] was at its peak. Under the haze of the biting weather, students, workers, and other people were engaged in a variety of chores, milling up and down the ever busy academic block of the Faculty of Arts, University of Lagos. Amidst the flow of human traffic on the corridors[56] of this sprawling edifice, the music department occupies its own distinct space. Within the confines of one of the lecturers' room, is a woman of substance, Dr. (Mrs.) Joy Nwosu Lo-Bamijoko, the Head of the Department of Music, who is a luminary figure in the academic world of music. Her office is moderately furnished. There is a mini-library stocked predominantly with music literature. To the left side of Lo-Bamijoko's table is a baby upright piano. Adjacent to the piano is a chalkboard that flourishes some lyrical verses. Lo-Bamijoko's cherubic face radiates life and simplicity. Her mien portrays a personality with unrestrained humble disposition. Here sits a towering figure in the academic community, an illustrious don that has entered many books of *Who is Who in Nigeria* and the Commonwealth.

Lo-Bamijoko's love for the growth of music industry in Nigeria has led to the birth of a scholarly journal, *Music in Nigeria* that she edits. Under the klieg lights, she has also staged several live performances in Italy, England, and the United States. Back at home, she was one of the few that pioneered female performances in the country. For almost two decades (1972-1992), this acclaimed music teacher performed regularly on television as a singer on music programs. She gleefully reminisced: "I was among those that opened the floodgate to female performers in Nigeria." Born fifty-two years ago in Enugu, Lo-Bamijoko's decision

54   Richard Mofe-Damijo, "Woman of Substance—Joy Nwosu: Singer, Critic, and Teacher, is Angry with Nigerian Society," *National Concord*, Monday, 13 February, 1989.

55   Harmattan is the coolest season of the year in Nigeria. It consists of dry, dusty air and cooler temperature. It starts in December and ends in January or February of every year.

56   Corridor = hallway

to take music as a career was influenced by her family setting—her parents were prominent members of the church choir. She grew up as a chorister. Lo-Bamijoko cut her first teeth in the glamorous world of music when she took part as a soloist in the then Eastern Nigerian Festival of Arts in 1957. At the festival, she won a certificate of merit as the best soloist for soprano voice. She won this coveted prize for the next four consecutive years.[57]

---

57   Tunde Thomas, "A Day with Joy Nwosu Lo-Bamijoko," *Daily Times*, Saturday, 20 February, 1993.

Epilogue

Joy Nwosu Lo-Bamijoko's stunning career falls within the parameters of intercultural musicology. It explicates the imprint of the tertian cultures Joy encountered during her musical training and professional experiences in Nigeria, Italy, and the United States. Indeed, this trifecta constitutes the definitive components of the total gamut of her musical out-puts. First, Joy's operatic singing reminisce the European classical training she received in Italy; second, her popular music style, that she calls folk songs, is influenced by the ethnomusicological training she received from the University of Michigan, African-American jazz, West African highlife music, and Igbo traditional music from southeast Nigeria; and third, Joy's personal vocal repertoire and songs she taught her students at the University of Lagos, consist of songs from the ternion cultures. Joy was the most hardworking and most productive amongst her female pairs in Nigeria; with interests covering the entire spectrum of artistic milieu including teaching, mammoth performances, research, recordings, and broadcasting. In addition to her inundating career, Joy found time to raise three wonderful children. Joy's astonishing contributions to the music industry in Nigeria is unparalleled to any other female musician.

When writing about Joy's life, we cannot shy away from her struggle to liberate Nigerian women from men's hegemony, and her audacity for voicing out stalwart opinions on controversial matters such as her stance on volatile political issues, in a nation where one could easily loose one's life and job for castigating the government or eminent personalities. Joy uses some of her pop songs like "The Call," to decry the relegation of Nigerian women to the bedroom and the kitchen. She was very independent and bodacious.

Joy deserves commendation for her resiliency in the face of all oppositions from her male contemporaries. Her assailants made several attempts to stop Joy by placing ridiculous obstacles in her way, but she always had a breakthrough, and prevailed. Joy was humiliated and knocked down many times, but she always bounce back triumphantly. Joy was indeed a victorious warrior—Tried and true. Not only did she defeat her enemies, she also witnessed some of them cascade from their lofty heights into the pit of despair and mausoleum. Sadly in retrospect, the only realm her adversaries were able to permanently mutilate Joy was to stop her from clinching the highest academic rank—the full professorship, that Joy rightly deserved and unequivocally qualified. The dream of everyone going into the academia was to soar to the pinnacle of the rank; for Joy, that dream was shattered by callous men. One could imagine the crushing blow of such a heart wrenching act in Joy's psychic. Suffice it to say, the tumultuous story of Joy could definitively be summed up as a perfect storm of catastrophic misfortunes, interlaced with spectacular victories.

We cannot discuss Joy's saga without referencing her faith in God that vividly anchored her throughout her entire challenging career. Her introduction to the Christian Faith at an early age by her parents, the convent school she attended at Enugu, and the conservatory training in Italy; all played a vital role in helping Joy to surmount caustic mountains she encountered at various stages of her herculean odyssey. Throughout the boisterous imbroglios, Joy found solace in the Lord, who stood by her and delivered her from the venomous furnaces often ignited by the so called pundits. Joy constantly fortified herself with unceasing prayer in the presence of the Lord, who annihilated the works of her detractors. Accordingly, at the end of the day, at the curtain call, when all is said and done, Joy gladly proclaims: "In all my problems, in all my travails, I trusted in the Lord, and the Lord delivered me from all of them."

References

Akatakpo, Gladys. "Joy Nwosu: People's Taste for Music." *Lagos Life*, Thursday, 23 April and Wed, 29 April, 1987.

Bozimo, Willy. "Joy Nwosu: A Music Star and an Ivory Tower." *Lagos Weekend*, Friday, 18 March, 1977.

Dominic, Joseph. "Joy Nwosu at the National Theater." *The Guardian*, Wednesday, 20 November, 1985.

Iloegbunam, Chucks. "Music Conversation with Joy Nwosu." *The Guardian*, Wednesday, 20 November, 1985.

Lo-Bamijoko, Joy Nwosu. *Mirror of Our Lives: Voices of Four Igbo Women*. Bloomington, IN: iUniverse Publishing, 2011.

—. "Music Education in Nigeria." *Nigeria Magazine* 150 (1984): 40-47.

—. "Performance Practice in Nigerian Music." *Black Perspective in Music* 2, No. 12 (Spring 1984): 3-20.

—. "Classification of Igbo Musical Instruments." *Nigeria Magazine*, No. 144 (1983): 38-58.

—. "Tuning Methods of African Musical Instruments: Some Examples from Nigeria and Ghana." *Nigeria Magazine*, No. 142 (1982): 15-24.

—. "A Preliminary Study of the Classification, Tuning and Educational Implications of the Standardization of Musical Instruments in Africa: The Nigerian Case." Ph.D. Dissertation, University of Michigan—Ann Arbor, 1981.

Mofe-Damijo, Richard. "Woman of Substance—Joy Nwosu: Singer, Critic, and Teacher, is Angry with Nigerian Society." *National Concord*, Monday, 13 February, 1989.

Oyewale, Femi. "She's a Joy to Hear." *Daily Times*, 1978.

Sadoh, Godwin. *Intercultural Dimensions in Ayo Bankole's Music*. New York: iUniverse Publishing, 2007.

Saunders, Leslie R. "Conversation on African Music: Leslie R. Saunders Interviews Joy Nwosu Lo-Bamijoko." *Music Educators Journal* 71, No. 9 (1985): 57-59.

Thomas, Tunde. "A Day with Joy Nwosu Lo-Bamijoko." *Daily Times*, Saturday, 20 February, 1993.

Uzoigwe, Joshua. *Akin Euba: An Introduction to the Life and Music of a Nigerian Composer*. Bayreuth: Eckhard Breitinger, 1992.

"Joy Nwosu Performs." *National Concord*, Saturday, 26 October, 1985.

"Eight-Hour Concert Billed for Independence Anniversary." *New Nigeria*, Saturday, 28 September, 1985.

"Joy Nwosu Sings for Nigeria." *The Guardian Supplement*, Sunday, 22 September, 1985.

"Joy's Christmas Treat." *Daily Times*, 17 December, 1983.

"Joy is a Thriller Any Day." *Daily Times,* Thursday, 22 December, 1977.

"Night of Folk Music and Excitement." *Evening Times,* Tuesday, 19 October, 1976.

Online Sources

"Joy Nwosu Lo-Bamijoko: A Nigerian Music Icon and Trailblazer."

http://www.uni-hildesheim.de/ntama

Joy Nwosu's Scholarly Publications

Books

Mirror of Our Lives: The Voices of Four Igbo Women. Bloomington, IN: iUniverse Publishing, 2011.

"A Preliminary Study of the Classification, Tuning and Educational Implications of the Standardization of Musical Instruments in Africa: The Nigerian Case." Ph.D. Dissertation, University of Michigan—Ann Arbor, 1981.

Cinema E Africa Nera. Rome: Edizione Tindalo, 1969.

Io Odio, Tu Odi. Rome: Edizione Tindalo, 1968.

Articles

"I Come from Utopia." *African Voices* (Spring/Summer, 2007): 18.

"Godwin Sadoh's Choral Works." *The Diapason* 98, No. 1 (January 2007): 16-17.

"New Hymn Book." *The Diapason* 97, No. 7 (July 2006): 19.

"Art Singing in Nigeria: The Composers and the Performers." In *African Art Music in Nigeria: Fela Sowande Memorial,* ed. Mosunmola Omibiyi-Obidike, 70-76. Ibadan, Nigeria: Stirling-Horden, 2001.

"C.M.A. and Induction Course for Music Teachers." *Music in Nigeria* 1, No. 4 (1993).

"Does African Classical Music Exist?" *Music in Nigeria* 1, No. 4 (1993).

"Music Notes: Music Materials." *Music in Nigeria* 1, No. 3 (1992).

"Basic Concepts in Music." *Music in Nigeria* 1, No. 1 (1991).

"Let Us Put the Records Right." *Music in Nigeria* 1, No. 2 (1991).

"The Humanities and National Development in Nigeria." Nelson Publication, 1991.

"Nigeria Can't Run Away from a Music School." *All Nigerian Food and Music Festival.* 1991: 52-54, 75-77.

"Social and Cultural Functions of Musical Instruments in Africa." *Third World First* 1, No. 1 (1990): 42-47.

"Music Education in Nigeria: The Status of Music Learning and Teaching." *The Quarterly* 1, No. 4 (Winter, 1990): 38-42.

"An Appraisal of 25 Years of Music Education in Nigeria: Its Impact On The Music of Nigeria."

"Music in Nigeria: 28 Years Later." *Nigeria Handbook Review* (1988): 167-171.

"Music in Nigeria." *Nigeria Magazine* (1987): 218-221.

"Classification of Igbo Musical Instruments." *African Music* (1987): 19-41.

"Leslie Saunders in Conversation with Joy Nwosu Lo-Bamijoko on African Music." *Music Educators Journal* 71, No. 9 (May, 1985): 57-59.

"Music Education in Nigeria." *Nigeria Magazine,* 150 (1984): 40-47.

"Performing Practice in Nigerian Music." *The Black Perspective* 12, No. 1 (Spring, 1983): 3-20.

"Classification of Nigerian Musical Instruments." *Nigeria Magazine,* (1983): 38-48.

"Tuning Methods of African Musical Instruments." *Nigeria Magazine,* 142 (1982): 15-26.

Features

"All Hands Must Be On Deck." *Music in Nigeria* 1, No. 4 (1993): 20.

"The Genesis of Children of Africa: A Post-mortem." *Music in Nigeria* 1, No. 3 (1992): 3-7.

"Music Promotions in Nigeria." *Music in Nigeria* 1, No. 3 (1992): 14 & 15-16.

"What is a Music Industry?" *Megastar* (March, 1989): 37.

"Music Industry: Problems of Management." *Megastar* (Feb., 1989): 28.

"Where is Nigeria's Music Industry?" *Megastar* (Jan., 1989): 21.

"Does Nigeria Have a Music Industry?" *Megastar* (Nov./Dec., 1988): 51-52.

"The Mmanwu Drama." *Megastar* (August, 1988): 34.

"Is There a Music Industry in Nigeria?" *Megastar* (July, 1988): 36-37.

"A Meditation Upon a Festival." *Megastar* (May, 1988): 45.

"Which Way Nigerian Music: A Case for a School of Music." *Megastar* (April, 1988): 32.

"Which Way Nigerian Music: Dialogue with the Deaf." *Megastar* (March, 1988): 39-40.

"Which Way Nigerian Music?" *Megastar* (Feb., 1988): 25.

"Youth Music in Nigeria." *Megastar* (Oct., 1987): 29-30, (Nov.,/Dec., 1987): 28-30, (Jan., 1988): 39-40.

"The Influence of Nigerian Folk Music on Modern Music." *Megastar* (Sept., 1987): 38-39.

"Music and Recreation." *Megastar* (June, 1987): 38 & 39.

"Understanding Music." *Megastar* (April, 1987): 39-40.

Joy Nwosu's List of Songs

Since her first and favourite instrument is voice, Joy writes exclusively vocal music. Below is a list of Joy's songs with short notes:

Songs

Uwam - means, My World! It is more of an exclamation than a statement.

Mathias Nwa Igwenegbu - Mathias, son of the man who killed millions. The Biafrans made a bomb that killed millions of people; this song was in honour of that bomb.

The Call - In my village, Enugwu-Ukwu, in Anambra State, we use ululation early in the mornings to rally our friends together to go to the stream. This was an ululation of anger, against what the war has done.

Egu Umu Agbogho - The Maidens Dance. I wrote this in the style of our traditional maiden dances.

Azania - This was the war cry of the South African blacks as they fought for freedom. Azania actually means Freedom; I dedicate the song to freedom.

Egwu Ubo - The music of the thumb piano.

Egwu Oyoyo - Oyoyo's beauty's dance, similar to Egwu Umu Agbogho, but this is a solo dance.

Ife di N'Oba - Wonders happen in Oba; Oba is a town in Anambra State. This is a story song about a wayward girl.

Prison Song - When I was young, I lived near a prison, and I heard the prisoners sing as they worked. This song is a recreation of what the prisoners sang.

Opera

Ogbanje Folk Opera.

Discography

The following are Joy Nwosu's songs recorded on commercial LPs in Nigeria:

EMI Records (1972)
Uwam - My World
Egwu Umu-Agbogho - The Maiden Dance
Iwe - The Call
Mathias Nwa Igwenegbu - Mathias Son of Thunder

Tabansi Records (1975)
Okwu - Words, and What They Can Do
Nne bu nne - Nothing Like Mother
Okwudili - Let it Be
Ozoemenam - Never Again!
Onu Uwa - Wicked World
Onyimu-O - My Friend!

Afrodisia Records (1977)

Azania - Freedom
Egwu Ubo - The Song of the Thumb Piano

Egwu Oyoyo - Oyoyo's Dance
The Love Game
Ife di N'Oba - Things Happen in Oba
The Prison Song
Ile - What the Tongue Can Do

Collection of Television Video Tapes
Voices – NTV 10, 1974
Artist Showcase – NTV 10, 1975
NBC Cultural Night - NTV 10, 1976
FESTAC 77 (Nigerian Contemporary) – NTA 10, 1977
Show Unlimited – NTA 10, 1978

Some of these tracks are now available on Amazon and iTunes.

Concert Programs

AFRICAN MUSIC:
A NIGERIAN EXPERIENCE

A PERFORMANCE/DEMONSTRATION BY
JOY NWOSU LO-BAMIJOKO

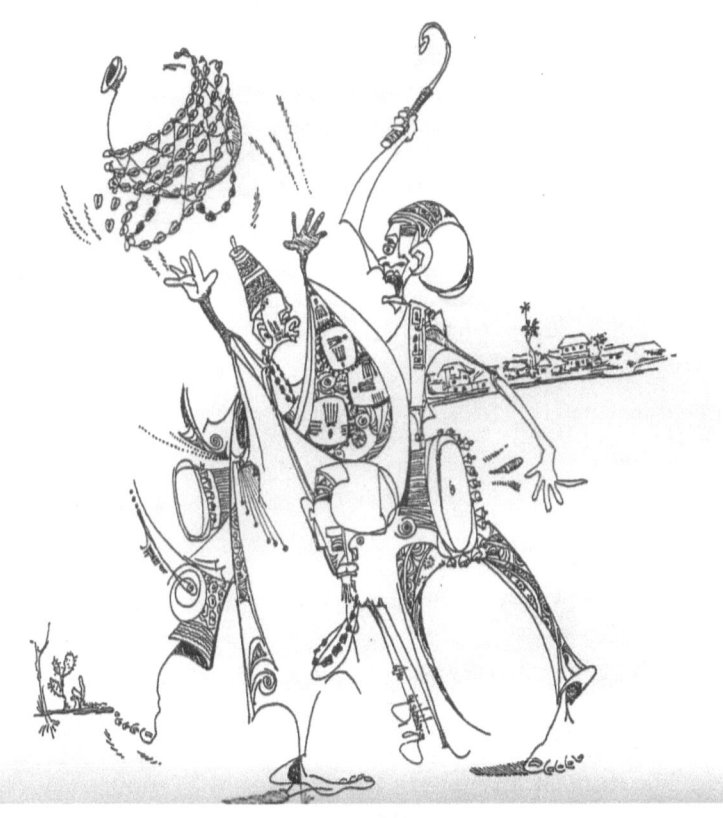

**African Music: A Nigerian Experience, Performance/
Demonstration by Joy Nwosu Lo-Bamijoko, at the University of
Michigan, School of Education Building, 1979.**

NIGERIA INSTITUTE OF SURVEYORS INTERNATIONAL SYMPOSIUM

OPENING CEREMONY — MONDAY OCTOBER 4TH 1982 — UNIVERSITY OF LAGOS
AUDITORIUM)

Director of Ceremony — Mr. O. Adebekun

10.00 a.m. — All delegates to be seated — Procession to high table.

NATIONAL ANTHEM: — Arranged and performed (on piano) by *Ngozi F. Chinwah

NATIONAL PLEDGE: — Read by Mrs. Adekoya

Music	Ave Maria	— Franz Schubert (1779 – 1826)
	Soprano	— *Dr. Joy Nwosu Lo-Bamijoko; Piano —Ngozi F. Chinwah.
	Welcome Address	— Vice Chancellor, University of Lagos.
	Civic Welcome	— Kabiyesi, Oba Adeyinka Oyekan
	Welcome Address:	— Chief R. Oluwole Coker, President, Nigerian Institute of Surveyors

	Official Opening of	
	Symposium	— Dr. Joseph Wayas, President of the Senate
Music		— I know that my redeemer liveth — Handel (1685–1759)
		— Jesu Joy of Men's Desiring — J.S. Bach (1685–1750)
		— (Arranged for piano by Ngozi F. Chinwah)
	Soprano	— Dr. Joy Nwosu Lo-Bamijoko; Piano — Ngozi F. Chinwah
	Keynote Address	— Prof E. Acquaye, President (CASLE)
	Vote of Thanks	— Bosun Ayinde, Secretary General NIS.
		— National Anthem

(All delegates remain standing, special guests depart.)
*Faculty members, Department of Music — University of Lagos.

**Nigeria Institute of Surveyors International Symposium Concert,
at the University of Lagos Auditorium, 1982.**

COMMAND PERFORMANCE

MARATHON SHOW

By

ANAMBRA STATE COUNCIL FOR ARTS AND CULTURE

Starring

JOY NWOSU

ZEAL ONYIA   JOE KING KOLOGBO
EDDY OKONTA   ONYEKAOZURU EZE
RICHARD BUCKNOR   DANIEL KORANTENG (JB)
BOLA JOHNSON (JB)

MARATHON SHOW INITIATED by Joy Nwosu is Anambra State Council for Arts and Culture input into the 27th National Day Celebration. The concert is divided into three (3) parts.

The first part embodies classical music selected from popular art songs by Nigeria and Western composers, as well as from the operas.

The second part consists of historical survey of popular music in Nigeria since Independence. Joy Nwosu will sing Nigerian favourites song with composers of some of those favourite songs.

The third part centres mainly on folksongs by Joy Nwosu herself and will include some of her most beautiful and thought provoking compositions.

SEQUENCE OF PRESENTATION AND SYNOPSIS OF TITLE SONGS

The following scenes will feature in the programmes—

Programme One

SCENE I.—PARIS

Addio, Del Passato Bei Sogni Ridenti—from La Traviate by Guiseppe Verdi (Violetta, the wayward one, falls in love with Alfredo Germont. Alfredo's father Giorgio Germont asks Violetta to give up his son, as his daughter's engagement is threatened by the association. Reluctantly, she agrees, and writes to tell Alfredo that she has fallen in love with Baron Douphol. Alfredo plays, and wins at card from the Baron, insults Violetta publicly. Violetta is dying of consumption when Alfredo returns to beg for forgiveness . . .).

SCENE II.—OPOBO T.

So Ri NA TEMEBO—from opu jaja by Adam Feberesin's (King Jaja, Prince Jaja and a representative of the British Council are seen discussing when Jaja's wife walks in a regal manner to warn her husband about the impending danger on the island.

SCENE III.—BETHLEHEM

A Night In Bethlehem—by Laz Ekwueme. Mary sat Her Orchard—from Night of Miracles by Ayo Bankole. (Mary sits in a loose gown, in the orchard sorting seeds, when Angel of the Lord appeared to her. A voice is heard off stage, recounting the incident as it occurs . . .

SCENE IV

The Lord's Prayer by Albert Hay Malotte.

Soprano ..   .. Joy Nwosu
Pianist ..   .. Richard Bucknor

Programme Two

This programme consists of historical coverage of popular music in Nigeria. Hits to be rendered include—

1. Another story by Israel Nwoba.
2. Bottom Belly by Herbert C.
3. Vik nyem Afumo by Zeal Onyia.
4. Oriwo by Eddy Okonta.
5. Love Adure by Rex Lawson.
6. One pound no balance by Osita Osadebe.
7. Baby Pancake by Kologbo.
8. Palavar — by Fela Anikulapo Kuti.

Programme Three

This will highlight scenes from every day life as composed by Joy Nwosu including—

1. *Ife oma Melu* (Our Lord's Prayer).
2. *Chim Atugolum Olu Ebube* (God has done great things for me).

27th National Day Celebration Command Performance at Government House Tennis Court, Enugu, 1987.

PROGRAMME

UNIVERSITY ANTHEM
THE UNIVERSITY OF IBADAN CHOIR AND ALL.

AVE MARIA — BACH-GOUNOD
AUTUMN THOUGHTS — GRIEG
EBBEN NE ANDRO LONTANA — CATALANI
(LA WALLY)

JOY NWOSU LO-BAMIJOKO — SOPRANO
RICHARD BUCKNOR — ACCOMPANIST.

EINE KLEINE NACHTMUSIK K. 525 — MOZART
ALLEGRO
ANDANTE
ALLEGRETTO

AJIBOLA MESIDA — VIOLIN
RICHARD BUCKNOR — ACCOMPANIST.

BALLADE NO. 3 IN A FLAT MAJOR OP. 47 — CHOPIN
BALLADE NO. 4 IN F MINOR OP. 52 — CHOPIN
YA ORULE – THEME AND VARIATIONS — AYO BANKOLE (SNR)
FOR LITTLE AYO

AYO BANKOLE (JNR) — PIANO.

SI TRA I CEPPI — HANDEL
BOIS EPAIS (SOMBRE WOODS) — LULLY
NOW PHOEBUS SINKETH IN THE WEST — ARNE
SAY GOODBYE NOW TO PASTIME — MOZART
AND PLAY, LAD
(THE MARRIAGE OF FIGARO)

CHRISTOPHER OYESIKU — BASS
AMORELLE INANGA — ACCOMPANIST.

THE PEASANT CANTATA — JOHANN SEBAS
(1685-17
ARRANGED BY
HARRY EDGAR

JOY NWOSU LO—BAMIJOKO —
MICHAEL HUDSON —
THE UNIVERSITY OF IBADAN CHOIR
CHRISTOPHER OYESIKU — Conductor
EMMANUEL BOAMAH — Accompanis

OVERTURE:

CHORUS. GOOD NEIGHBOURS ALL.
RECIT. COME, KITTY
CHORUS. SPRING COMES LAUGHING
RECIT. (BASS) OUR MASTER WE ALL RESPECT
ARIA, (BASS) OF THE FACTOR YOU HAD BES
RECIT. (SOPRANO) ENOUGH OF HIM!
ARIA. (SOPRANO) HAPPY IS THE LAND.
RECIT. OUR MASTER THINKS OF OLD A
CHORUS. GOOD CAUSE HAVE WE.
RECIT, (BASS) AND NOW I ASK YOU ALL
RECIT (SOPRANO) FIFTY FLORINS SEEM A LOT.
RECIT (SOPRANO) ONE MOMENT, PLEASE!
ARIA. (SOPRANO) OF FLOWERS THE FAIREST.
RECIT. (BASS) THANK GOODNESS THAT IS OVE
CHORUS IF FORTUNE HAD MADE ME THE
RECIT. (SOPRANO) AND I WERE THE LADY SO FAIR
CHORUS. (FEMALE VOICES) HEY DERRY, DOWN DERRY.
RECIT. (BASS) PERHAPS YOU'RE RIGHT!

**University of Ibadan Concert of Choral and Instrumental Music,
at the Trenchard Hall, 1989.**

Programme

AYO BANKOLE (Jnr) .... PIANO

Theme and variations for little Ayo) The late
Ya Orule) Ayo Bankole

Variations on Yoruba Air .... Ayo Bankole (Jnr).

The Golliwogs Cakewalk .... Claude Debussy

MICHELLE SCHARAPAN.........PIANO

Sonata in a minor K 310 .... W. A. Mozart

Three Klavierstucke (posthumous) D 946 .... F. Schubert

TIMI OKARA .... SOPRANO

Ayo Bankole .... (accompanist)

Ozu Kombo .... **A. FIBERESIMA**

JOY NWOSU LO-BAMIJOKO .... SOPRANO

Richard Bucknor .... (accompanist)

To Daffodils .... Frederick Deluis
Nebbie .... Ottorino Respighil
Toujours .... Gasriel Faure
Ritorna Vinciter .... Giuseppe Verdi

MICHELLE SCHARAPAN .... PIANO

Two Rhapsodies OP 79 (B minor and G minor) .... J. Brahms

Suite OP IX .... B. Bartok

Interlude/Cocktails

Classical Music Concert—A Night of Excellence, Sponsored by Elf Nigeria Limited, at Lagos and Port-Harcourt, 1989.

UNIVERSITY OF LAGOS
CENTRE FOR CULTURAL STUDIES

MUSIC UNIT

PRESENTS

A VOICE RECITAL

By

JOY NWOSU LO-BAMIJOKO

On

FRIDAY 6, APRIL 1990

In

The   University Auditorium

At 7 p.m.

ADMISSION:- ₦5.00 Flat or by Special
Invitation

**University of Lagos Center for Cultural Studies Concert, at the
University Auditorium, 1990.**

Otunba T. O. Shobowale Benson, CFR, SAN.

Presents

Joy Nwosu

in

Concert

For the Promotion of Classical Music

At the

Nigerian Institute of International Affairs
13/15, Kofo Abayomi Road,
Victoria Island, Lagos

October 26, 1990

At 6.00 - 7.30 p.m.

Otunba T. O. Shobowale Benson Presents Joy Nwosu in Concert,
at the Nigerian Institute of International Affairs, Lagos, 1990.

THE CHOIR

of

ST. PAUL'S ANGLICAN CHURCH, IGBORE, ABEOKUTA

PRESENTS

CHRISTMAS CONCERT FEATURING

(i) THE CHOIR
(ii) PERFORMING GUEST ARTISTES

1. Laz Ekwueme
2. Joy Nwosu Lo-Banjoko
3. Ajibola Meshida
4. Richard Femi Bucknor

on

Saturday, 1st December 1990 at 5.30 p.m.

UNDER THE DISTINGUISHED CHAIRMANSHIP OF

CHIEF OLURANTI SONEYE
Lukotun Parakoyi of Igbore

SPECIAL GUEST OF HONOUR

OTUNBA E. J. OGUNBANKE
The Balogun of Ala, Maiyegun of Igbore

LIFE GRAND PATRON AND FATHER OF THE DAY
OBA MOFOLORUNSO OYEBADE LIPEDE I
The Alake of Egbaland

VEN. V. O. SOTUNDE
Vicar

REV. A. ABODUNRIN
Curate

Christmas Concert by the Choir of Saint Paul's Anglican Church, Abeokuta, 1990.

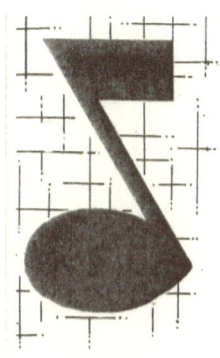

IDEAS COMMUNICATIONS LTD

PRESENTS

The Best in Classical Music

THE CITY CHORALE

in the performance of the
ORATORIO-- "THE CREATION"

BY JOSEPH HADYN

Featuring great Nigerian Classical Singers

JOY NWOSU (SOPRANO)
LAZ EKWUEME (TENOR)
CHRISTOPHER OYESIKU (BASS)
RICHARD BUCKNOR (PIANO)
KAYODE ONI (ORGAN)

EMEKA NWOKEDI SENATOR 'LERE ADESINA
Music Director/Conductor Group Leader

VENUE: L'HOTEL EKO MERIDIEN, V.I LAGOS.
DATE: SUNDAY 7TH JULY, 1991
TIME: 7 P.M PROMPT
ADMISSION- INVITATION/TICKETS N200
(Available at JAZZ 38, USIS, GATE)

Supported by:

BENSON & HEDGES
MUSIC

Bringing music to your life

The City Chorale in the Performance of the Oratorio, *The Creation* by Joseph Haydn, at L'Hotel Eko Meridien, Lagos, 1991.

PROGRAMME

National Anthem
Where'er You Walk
(Semele) .... Handel
Arranged for S.A.T.B. by Thomas Keighley

My Bonnie Lass .... John Brydson
Far Away .... Arranged for S.A.T.B. by Arthur Pearson

God's Gonna Buil' Up Zion's Wall .... Jester Hairston

University of Ibadan Choir
Christopher Oyesiku—Conductor
Adeniran Obasa—Piano

♪ ♪ ♪

La Walli .... Verdi *Catalani*
Pace, Pace Mio Dio
(La Forza Del Destino) .... Verdi
To Daffodils .... Delius
Ogene .... Lawrence Emeka

Joy Nwosu Lo-Bamijoko—Soprano
Richard Bucknor—Piano

♪ ♪ ♪

Sonatina in D Op.36. No.6
Allegro Con Spirito
Rondo—Allegro Spiritoso .... Clementi
Arabesque No.1 in E Major .... Debussy
Andaluza No.5 in E Minor .... Granados

Joyce Lowe—Piano

♪ ♪ ♪

INTERVAL — 15 MINUTES

When the Night Wind Howls
(Ruddigore) .... Sullivan
Recit: Che Mai Vegg'io?
Aria: Infelice, E Tu Credevi
(Ernani) .... Verdi
Come into the Garden Maud .... Balfe
The Lost Chord .... Sullivan

Michael Hudson—Baritone
Joyce Lowe—Piano

♪ ♪ ♪

Rondo Capriccioso Op.14 .... Mendelssohn

Amorelle Inanga—Piano

♪ ♪ ♪

Love, Fare Thee Well .... Brahms
Orisa bi Ofun Kosi .... Ayo Bankole
Eje K'a S'ise O .... Dayo Dedeke
Ojo Maro .... Ayo Bankole

University of Ibadan Choir
Christopher Oyesiku—Conductor
Adeniran Obasa—Piano

Rotary International District 9130 Nigeria in Collaboration with Music Circle of the University of Ibadan, Presents a Musical Evening, at the Trenchard Hall, University of Ibadan, 1992.

Other Books by Godwin Sadoh

Christopher Oyesiku: Preeminent Nigerian Choral Conductor

Thomas Ekundayo Phillips: The Doyen of Nigerian Church Music

Samuel Akpabot: The Odyssey of a Nigerian Composer-Ethnomusicologist

The Organ Works of Fela Sowande: Cultural Perspectives

Intercultural Dimensions in Ayo Bankole's Music

Joshua Uzoigwe: Memoirs of a Nigerian Composer-Ethnomusicologist

E Korin S'Oluwa: Fifty Indigenous Christian Hymns from Nigeria